2nd Edition
Ventures 5
WORKBOOK

Gretchen Bitterlin ▪ **Dennis Johnson** ▪ **Donna Price** ▪ **Sylvia Ramirez**

K. Lynn Savage (Series Editor)

CAMBRIDGE
UNIVERSITY PRESS

CAMBRIDGE
UNIVERSITY PRESS

University Printing House, Cambridge CB2 8BS, United Kingdom

One Liberty Plaza, 20th Floor, New York, NY 10006, USA

477 Williamstown Road, Port Melbourne, VIC 3207, Australia

314–321, 3rd Floor, Plot 3, Splendor Forum, Jasola District Centre, New Delhi – 110025, India

79 Anson Road, #06–04/06, Singapore 079906

Cambridge University Press is part of the University of Cambridge.

It furthers the University's mission by disseminating knowledge in the pursuit of education, learning and research at the highest international levels of excellence.

www.cambridge.org
Information on this title: www.cambridge.org/9781108450683

First published 2008
Second edition 2014

20 19 18 17 16 15 14 13 12 11 10 9 8 7 6 5

Printed in Malaysia by Vivar Printing

A catalogue record for this publication is available from the British Library

ISBN 978-1-108-44959-5 Student's Book
ISBN 978-1-108-44944-1 Online Workbook
ISBN 978-1-316-98669-1 Teacher's Edition
ISBN 978-1-108-44924-3 Class Audio CDs
ISBN 978-1-108-45050-8 Presentation Plus

Additional resources for this publication at www.cambridge.org/ventures

Front cover photography by RichVintage/E+/Getty Images.
Back cover photography by pressureUA/iStock/Getty Images Plus/Getty Images; Adidet Chaiwattanakul/EyeEm/Getty Images; pixelfit/E+/Getty Images.
Audio produced by CityVox.

CONTENTS

UNIT 1 SELLING YOURSELF

Lesson A Listening

1 Read the statements. Listen to the lecture and circle *T* (true) or *F* (false).

1. Hard skills include personal qualities and "people skills." T (F)
2. An example of a people skill is communicating well with co-workers. T F
3. Using a cash register is an example of a soft skill. T F
4. Hard skills and soft skills are both important. (T) F
5. The speaker thinks that hard skills are more important than soft skills. T F
6. Soft skills are harder to teach than hard skills. T F

2 Complete this excerpt from the lecture. Then listen again and check your answers.

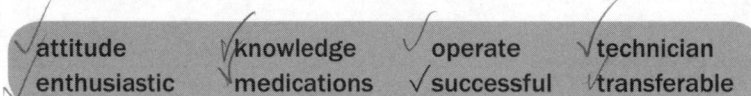

✓attitude	✓knowledge	✓operate	✓technician
✓enthusiastic	✓medications	✓successful	✓transferable

. . . Basically, there are two types of skills you will need if you want to be ___successful___.
                                                                                      1
The first type is called "hard skills," and the second type is called "soft skills."

"Hard skills" are the technical skills and the ___Knowledge___ you need in order to do
                                                     2
a job. These are things you can learn in school or on the job. For example, if you want to be a

pharmacy ___technician___, you will need to learn the names of ___medicatwns___, how to
             3   4
use a cash register, how to take messages from doctors, and so on. If your goal is to get a job in a

factory, then you need to learn how to use the machines and maybe how to ___operate___ a
                                                                                5
computer. These are hard skills.

"Soft skills" are a little harder to define. They include your personal qualities and what we call

your "people skills." For example, are you hardworking, motivated, reliable, and ___enthusiastic___?
                                                                                       6
Do you communicate well with your classmates and co-workers? Do customers like you and trust

you? Those are examples of soft skills.

Sometimes people ask me what's more important, hard skills or soft skills. Well, both of them

are important, but I think soft skills are probably more important because they're harder to teach

and because they are ___transferable___ . . . I mean, you can take them with you from job to job.
                          7
If you have a good ___attitude___ and you communicate well, you will be successful in any job
                        8
you have.

Lesson B Participial adjectives

Study the grammar explanation on page 4 of the *Transitions* Student's Book.

1 **Complete the sentences. Use the correct adjective.**

1. He thinks driving a race car is _____*exciting*_____.
   (excite)
2. The designers are _____ with their latest client.
   (frustrate)
3. Her job is very _____.
   (tire)
4. Lying in a hammock is _____.
   (relax)
5. John feels _____ because his work is not challenging.
   (bore)
6. She feels _____ at work. There's too much work to do!
   (annoy)

2 **Read the chart. Then complete the sentences about Jim and Bob.**

	Jim	Bob
Office work	doesn't like sitting for hours	likes working in a quiet place
Construction	enjoys building things	doesn't like physical work
Teaching	loves working with students	prefers to work alone

1. **Office work (bore, interest)**

   Jim thinks office work is _____*boring*_____ because he doesn't like sitting for hours.

   Bob is _____ in working in a quiet place.

2. **Construction (excite, tire)**

   Jim is _____ about working in construction. He enjoys building things.

   Bob gets _____ when he does this kind of work.

3. **Teaching (thrill, frighten)**

   Jim thinks working with students is _____. He loves to work with young people.

   Bob thinks working with students is _____. He prefers to work alone.

Lesson C Reading

1 Complete the sentences.

achieve   challenging   deadline   measure   realistic   √set

1. Lina has _____*set*_____ a goal for the future. She is interested in becoming a translator.

2. Lina wants to be a translator because she thinks the job will be _____. It won't be boring because it will require her to use her language skills.

3. In order to _____ her goal, Lina has made a plan. She has enrolled in a Spanish/English translation program at her local community college.

4. The program takes two years to finish. Lina's professors will _____ her progress by giving her tests and grading her homework.

5. In addition to taking classes, Lina wants to apply for a volunteer job at her daughter's school. She wants to translate for parents who don't speak English. The _____ for applying is tomorrow, so she needs to fill out the application today.

6. Lina knows she has set a _____ goal because her language skills are good. After she completes the translation program, she will probably be able to find a job as a translator in her community.

2 Look at the article "Setting Goals for the Future" on page 6 of the *Transitions* Student's Book. Answer the questions.

1. What is the main idea of the article? Circle the answer.

   a. Setting a goal means making a decision about what you want to achieve and deciding how to achieve it.

   b. Setting goals can help you get what you want in the future.

   c. Goals can be difficult to measure.

2. Supporting details are facts, opinions, examples, and other ideas that support the main idea. What are four details that support the main idea of the article?

   a. _The goal should be detailed._____

   b. _____

   c. _____

   d. _____

Lesson D Reading

1 **Circle the correct words.**

1. Lee is very (committed) / committing to his job – he often works overtime without complaining.

2. If you want to get promoted, showing **leadership / leading** is a good way to indicate to your boss that you would do well in a higher level position.

3. Vinh doesn't do well at his job because he can't **communication / communicate** easily with others in English.

4. Sandra got the job instead of the other candidates because she showed a lot of **mature / maturity** during her interview.

5. Ricardo was able to **analyzing / analyze** the problem and come up with a good solution to it.

6. What's the key to being **successful / success** at work?

7. Olga tried to make a good **impress / impression** at work, but she wasn't successful.

8. Companies value employees who are able to **recognize / recognition** problems, develop a plan for solving them, and follow through with that plan.

9. Because of Emily's skills at **analyzing / analyze** problems, she got the promotion.

10. Because his supervisor felt John lacked **committed / commitment**, John didn't get the promotion.

2 **Look at the article "Keys for Success at Work" on page 8 of the *Transitions* Student's Book. Complete the chart below. Skim the article by reading the bold subheadings to quickly find the information you need.**

What Employers Look For	
Skills or qualities	**Example of skills or qualities**
1. *Communication skills*	*get along well with others*
2.	
3.	
4.	
5.	
6.	

Lesson E Writing

1 **Read the paragraph. Complete the résumé.**

> Rachel Christie wants to get a job as a patient care technician or nurse's assistant at a hospital in Tucson, Arizona. She worked as a nurse in her home country of Mali before moving to Tucson. She has a nursing degree from the University of Bamako in Mali, and a high school diploma from the International School of Bamako. Rachel worked as a nurse at the Red Cross Hospital in Bamako from June 2014 to March 2017. In Tucson, she has volunteered in the pediatric unit at University Medical Center since April 2017. She has helped in the playroom and she also reads books to children. Rachel has a lot of skills for working in a hospital, and she has taken care of sick children for many years. She can also speak French and English fluently, and she gets along well with everyone.

Rachel Christie
66 Pine Street
Tucson, AZ 85719
(520) 555-4321
rc@cup.org

Objective

Education

Work Experience

Volunteer Experience

Skills

UNIT 2 BUILDING SELF-CONFIDENCE

Lesson A Listening

1 **Read the statements. Listen to the lecture and circle the main idea.**

1. David is positive, enthusiastic, and conscientious.

2. Your personality and how you feel about yourself can determine whether or not you get a promotion.

3. Sarah judges herself too harshly and, therefore, she will never get a promotion.

2 **Complete the lecture. Then listen again and check your answers.**

conscientious	√dedicated	judges	promotion
criticizes	disappointed	optimistic	responsibilities

I'd like to describe two different workers for you, David and Sarah, and while I'm talking about them I'd like you to think about which one is more likely to get a promotion. OK?

So, David and Sarah, they work together in a busy office. Both of them are ___*dedicated*___ (1) to their jobs; they're _____ (2) and loyal, but their personalities are very different. David is a motivated, _____ (3) person who enjoys taking on new challenges. It's true that sometimes he works too quickly and makes mistakes, but when this happens, he thinks of it as a learning experience and promises himself that he'll do better next time.

Now, Sarah, on the other hand, _____ (4) herself very negatively if she makes a mistake. Although she's really smart and works hard, she often worries that she is not doing a good job, and her feelings are easily hurt when anyone _____ (5) her. Sarah's expectations of herself are unrealistically high, so she's easily _____ (6).

OK, so, which worker do you think got the _____ (7)? David, obviously. He's happy and enthusiastic about his new _____ (8), while Sarah, yeah, as you can probably guess, feels like a failure.

Lesson B The present passive

Study the grammar explanation on page 14 of the *Transitions* Student's Book.

1 **Read the sentences. Circle the present passive form in each sentence.**

1. Jane feels she (is judged) too harshly by her boss.
2. She is affected by his criticism.
3. Jane is sometimes pressured to work overtime without pay.
4. Her co-workers are not required to stay after 5:00 p.m.
5. They are not asked to take on extra work.
6. Jane feels she is expected to do the work of two people.
7. She is stressed by the extra hours that she puts in.
8. Jane stays at the job because she is influenced by her parents. They tell her not to quit, so she doesn't.

2 **Read the sentences about the rules at Atlanta Vocational School. Rewrite them with the present passive.**

1. The school doesn't allow students to smoke in the buildings.

   Students are not allowed to smoke in the buildings.

2. The school doesn't permit food or drink in the computer lab.

   _____

3. The school requires a permit to park in the parking lot.

   _____

4. The school charges students a fee to use the gym.

   _____

5. The school provides guest passes to visitors.

   _____

6. The school expects students to meet with the counselor.

   _____

7. Teachers do not admit late students into class.

   _____

8. The school posts grades on a bulletin board in the hall.

   _____

Lesson C Reading

1 **Complete the chart with the correct word forms. More than one word may be possible.**

Noun	Verb	Adjective
motivation	motivate	*motivated, motivational*
criticism		
		influential, influenced
stress		
	succeed	
encouragement		
		judgmental
product		

2 **Look at the article "Understanding Self-Confidence" on page 16 of the *Transitions* Student's Book. Complete the outline. Write only the most important parts of the article.**

1. Topic: _Understanding self-confidence_

2. Definition of self-confidence: _____

3. Adjectives that describe a self-confident person: _____

   _____

4. Adjectives that describe a person without self-confidence: _____

   _____

5. What self-confidence is affected by: _____

   _____

6. Behaviors that show a lack of self-confidence:

   a. _____

   b. _____

   c. _____

   d. _____

   e. _____

Lesson D Reading

1 **Write the adjectives.**

-able   -al   -ious   -ive

1. conscience   _conscientious_   4. rely   _____

2. assert   _____   5. create   _____

3. loyalty   _____   6. cooperate   _____

Write the adjectives next to their definitions.

7. taking care to do things right   _____ _conscientious_

8. original and imaginative   _____

9. expressing oneself firmly   _____

10. faithful   _____

11. dependable   _____

12. willing to work together   _____

2 **Look at the article "Building Self-Confidence" on page 18 of the *Transitions* Student's Book. Skim the article. Read the title, the subheadings, and the first sentence in each paragraph. Then complete each statement.**

1. The article answers the question _How do you build self-confidence?_ _____

2. The second paragraph is about _____

3. The second section is about _____

4. The third paragraph is about self-confidence as a _____

5. The second section lists six _____ for success:

   a. Think about your good _____

   b. Think _____

   c. Set _____ _____

   d. Focus on _____, not _____

   e. Be _____

   f. Find a _____ _____ for self-expression.

Lesson E Writing

1 **Read the paragraph about Raymond. Complete the diagrams.**

> Raymond works at an electronics store. He is very interested in electronics, so he thought he would love working at this kind of store. When Raymond first started working there two years ago, the store managers found him to be very knowledgeable about electronics and motivated to help customers. Raymond was also very ambitious, and he wanted to be promoted to a managerial position as soon as possible. The owner of the store talked to Raymond and told him that he was impressed by his knowledge of the products in the store and how they work. However, he also told Raymond about some of the qualities that he would need to work on if he wanted to become a store manager. Raymond was told that he needed to work on being a better team player. Other workers had complained that he only liked to work by himself, that he was not very patient, and that he got annoyed when work at the store didn't go as planned. They also said that he was not very flexible and that he never wanted to work more than his regular hours. The owner told Raymond that if he worked on these issues, he might be able to get promoted in the future.

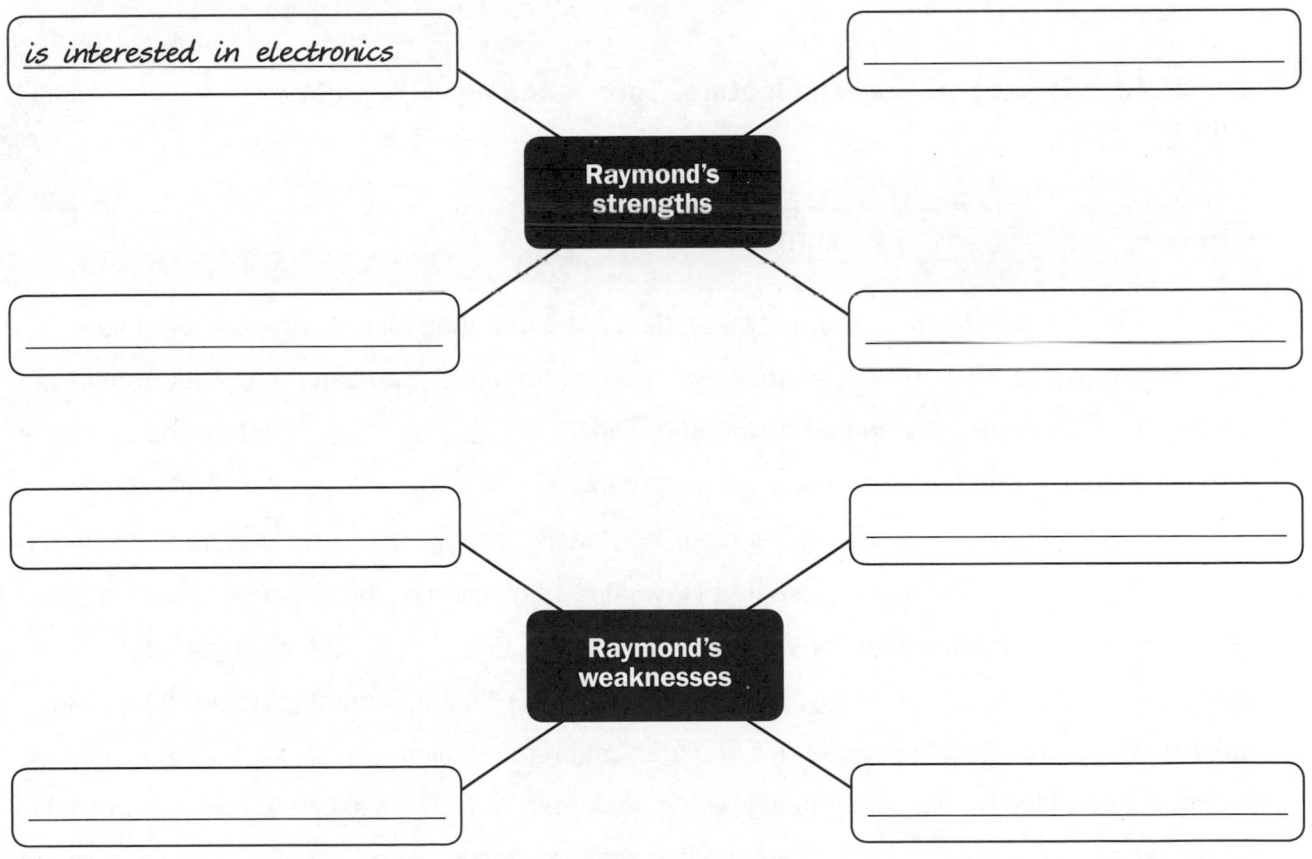

is interested in electronics

Raymond's strengths

Raymond's weaknesses

UNIT 3 VOLUNTEERING

Lesson A Listening

1 **Read the questions. Listen to the lecture and fill in the information below.**

1. Write two reasons why volunteering can be a very beneficial, or good, experience.

   a. _It is a type of on-the-job training._

   b. _____

2. Write four examples of volunteer jobs.

   a. _____   c. _____

   b. _____   d. _____

3. Write two examples of volunteer jobs you could do overseas, or in another country.

   a. _____

   b. _____

2 **Complete this excerpt from the lecture. Then listen again and check your answers.**

abilities	day-care	food bank	low-cost
✓beneficial	elderly	graffiti	training

. . . If you've ever volunteered anywhere, then you know that volunteering can be a very
_____beneficial_____ experience. Although you don't earn money, you can learn a lot about the
$\overset{}{1}$
world of work. Volunteering can be a type of on-the-job _____. Also, you can meet
$\overset{}{2}$
wonderful people and feel good about helping them.

There are all kinds of places to volunteer, and each place is looking for people with different
_____. If you are interested in working with children, you could become a tutor and
$\overset{}{3}$
help them with their homework, or volunteer in a _____ center. If you enjoy working
$\overset{}{4}$
with _____ people, you could volunteer your time in a nursing home. If you like
$\overset{}{5}$
building things, you could volunteer for an organization that builds _____ housing
$\overset{}{6}$
for people who don't have much money. Other volunteer work you might be interested in could
be removing _____ from public places, or working at a _____ to put
$\overset{}{7}$ $\overset{}{8}$
together food boxes or baskets for low-income families.

Lesson B Indirect (reported) speech

Study the grammar explanation on page 24 of the *Transitions* Student's Book.

1 Read the sentences and identify whether they are direct or indirect speech.

1. I like working with elderly people.   (direct)   indirect
2. Jane said that she enjoyed working outside.   direct   indirect
3. Bill mentioned that he volunteered at the food bank.   direct   indirect
4. Robin volunteers at the library.   direct   indirect
5. Sarah said that volunteering was good on-the-job training.   direct   indirect
6. James said that he volunteered at a preschool.   direct   indirect
7. Volunteering during college is a good idea.   direct   indirect

2 Change the direct statements to indirect statements.

1. "I want to volunteer at the library," said Abdul.
   Abdul said that he wanted to volunteer at the library.

2. "I'm studying to be a librarian," he said.
   _____

3. "I want to get on-the-job training," he mentioned.
   _____

4. "I'm interested in becoming a children's librarian at a public library," he added.
   _____

5. "I want to practice reading stories aloud to children," Abdul said.
   _____

6. "It's also a good way to improve my English-speaking skills," he said.
   _____

7. "I can put this volunteer experience on my résumé," he mentioned.
   _____

8. "I'm going to start out by shelving books at the library," Abdul told me.
   _____

9. "I think it will be a very interesting volunteer position," Abdul added.
   _____

Lesson C Reading

1 **Complete the story about Elizabeth.**

> collection   committed   passion   recruiting   supervises
> combine   √ coordinator   popularity   recycling   supports

Elizabeth is a volunteer ___coordinator___ at her local community college. She matches

people with volunteer work that they are interested in. Elizabeth is good at _____,
                                                                                    2

or attracting, new members. She advertises the positions in the college newspaper. In addition

to placing volunteers, Elizabeth _____ them, or oversees their work. Elizabeth has
                                            3

noticed that volunteering has risen in _____ recently; more and more people are
                                                4

calling her to ask about volunteer jobs.

Some of the volunteer work advertised through the community college involves

_____, or reusing items in a different way. Other positions involve the
          5

_____ of food for people who can't afford to buy food for their families.
          6

Some students try to _____ their studies with their volunteer work by working in
                              7

areas that relate to their classes. For example, education majors volunteer in schools.

Elizabeth loves her job because she sees a lot of volunteers doing their jobs with

_____, or a great love for what they do. Her volunteers are very _____
          8   9

to their jobs – in general, they show up on time and go in when they are needed. Elizabeth

_____ her volunteers – if there is ever a problem, she tries to help in any way that
          10

she can.

2 **Look at the article "Volunteering the Family Way" on page 26 of the _Transitions_
Student's Book. Complete the diagram below.**

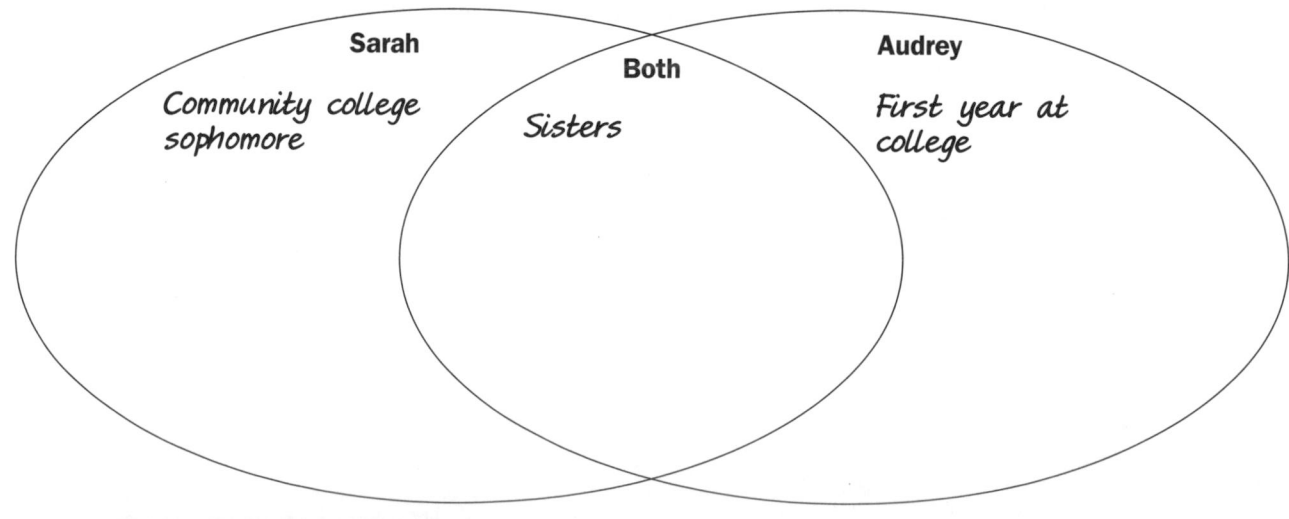

Sarah
Community college sophomore

Both
Sisters

Audrey
First year at college

Lesson D Reading

1 **Circle the correct words.**

1. If you participate in an event, you **are** / **are not** involved in it.

2. You **can** / **cannot** get college credit for volunteering at many colleges.

3. Helping an elderly neighbor **is** / **is not** an example of a good deed.

4. An advisor at a community college helps you with your **grades** / **schedule**.

5. Community service means helping people in your town by working **with** / **without** pay.

6. If an employer reads about the volunteering you have done and how helpful you've been to the community, it **should** / **shouldn't** help you get an interview.

7. Community service on your résumé shows that you **are** / **are not** curious about the world around you.

8. It **is** / **is not** common for volunteer work to relate to a student's major.

2 **Look at the article "Volunteering While at College" on page 28 of the *Transitions* Student's Book. Scan the article to find the following information.**

Topic sentence: _There are many benefits to volunteering while in college._

Transition 1: _First of all,_

Benefit 1: _____

Example 1: _____

Transition 2: _____

Benefit 2: _____

Example 2: _____

Transition 3: _____

Benefit 3: _____

Example 3: _____

Concluding sentence: _____

Lesson E Writing

1 Read the article "The Peace Corps." Complete the summary outline about the article.

The Peace Corps

The Peace Corps is a program that was started in the United States in 1961 by President John F. Kennedy. Kennedy asked Americans to promote peace and understanding by volunteering in developing countries. Since 1961, nearly 200,000 Peace Corps volunteers have lived and worked in 139 host countries around the world.

Americans of all ages can apply for the Peace Corps. Volunteers often have experience and education in areas such as language teaching, nursing, engineering, or business.

Most volunteers have at least a bachelor's degree and serve a term of two years.

Where each volunteer works depends on their experiences and interests and on the needs of the host country. Often they work in schools, hospitals, city offices, or in rural areas. They work side by side with people from the host country to help with and improve teaching, health services, the conditions in cities, and farming techniques.

Peace Corps volunteers learn another language, experience a new culture, and develop job and leadership skills. They may also bring their experience back to the United States and share it with their family and friends. The Peace Corps benefits not only the host countries, but also the volunteers.

1. Introduction: *The Peace Corps is a program that sends volunteers to work in developing countries. Its aim is to help countries with their needs and to help Americans learn about and understand other cultures.*

2. People who volunteer: _____

_____

3. Benefit for host country: _____

_____

4. Benefit for volunteer: _____

_____

5. Conclusion: _____

_____

UNIT 4 EFFECTIVE JOB APPLICATIONS

Lesson A Listening

1 **Read the steps. Then listen to the lecture and number the steps in the order you hear them.**

_____ ask previous employers for references   _____ start looking for jobs in your area

_____ you'll need to write a résumé   _____ filling out applications

_1_ deciding what type of job you want   _____ you may need to write a cover letter

Write the steps in the chart. Then listen again and write the transitional word or phrase you hear before each step.

Transitional phrases	Steps
1. The first step is	deciding what type of job you want.
2.	
3.	
4.	
5.	
6.	

2 **Listen to the lecture again. Listen for these excerpts and write the missing words.**

Step 1 . . . What are your interests? What are your hobbies? What are you good at? __What__ __kind__ __of__ experience __do__ __you__ __have__?
        1

Step 2 . . . One of the best ways to _____ _____ about job openings is by
                            2
_____ _____ _____ – you know, through talking to friends, neighbors, and
   3
family members.

Step 3 . . . For most jobs these days you can _____ _____ _____, or else you
                                        4
can go to the workplace itself. Fill out the job application carefully and _____ _____!
                                                        5

Step 4 . . . If you've never worked before, _____ ____ a trusted _____ or
                                        6
_____ who knows you well and would be a good personal reference for you.

Step 5 . . . We'll talk about _____ _____ at our _____ _____.
                                          7

Step 6 . . . A personalized letter that tells an employer how much you are _____ ____ the
                                                    8
job could make all the difference in getting an invitation for an interview.

Check your answers. See page 54.

Lesson B Past perfect

Study the grammar explanation on page 34 of the *Transitions* Student's Book.

1 **Complete the paragraph with the past perfect form of the verbs.**

Johanna thought her job interview went well. She felt that she ___*had prepared*___
(prepare) very thoroughly. She _____ (research) the company online,
and _____ (write) down some questions that she could ask about
the position. She _____ (fill) out the job application carefully, making
sure that she _____ (answer) all of the questions. Even though she
_____ (not work) for several years while she stayed at home with her young
children, she _____ (not leave) any gaps in her employment history. Instead, she
_____ (explain) why she _____ (not work) during those years.
Because Johanna _____ (do) so much preparation beforehand, she felt very
comfortable when she sat down for the interview.

2 **Read each set of events. Decide which happened first and which happened second. Then combine the two sentences. Use the past perfect for the first event.**

1. __*1*__ John worked for three years as a teacher's assistant.

   __*2*__ He got his teaching certificate.

   John had worked for three years as a teacher's assistant before *he got his teaching certificate*.

2. _____ John decided to apply for a job.

   _____ John saw many online ads for teachers.

   _____ when _____.

3. _____ Many people interviewed for the job.

   _____ John finally got an interview.

   By the time _____.

4. _____ John went to the interview.

   _____ John got good letters of recommendation from his previous employers.

   _____ before _____.

5. _____ The principal decided to hire John.

   _____ The principal read John's wonderful letters of recommendation.

   After _____.

Lesson C Reading

1 Complete the story about Giancarlo.

> applicants   cautious   √inexperienced   scammer
> beware   deception   realize

Giancarlo wants a job as a waiter but he is ___*inexperienced*___. He saw an ad online
                                                    1
asking for _____ for a job that required no experience. Giancarlo was excited
              2
because the salary was great, and he could work at home. The job description asked people
to assemble products at home. Giancarlo didn't know that it wasn't a real job; it was posted on
the Internet by a _____. Giancarlo didn't _____ that there were such
                     3   4
dishonest people on the Internet, so he applied for the job and sent in a check for $100. He
thought it was OK to send in $100 since he was going to make a great salary. When Giancarlo
didn't get a response, he asked his sister about the ad. She explained that you have to be
_____ when doing a job search on the Internet. She told Giancarlo that there
         5
is a lot of _____ on the Internet. People tell you things that aren't always true.
                6
Giancarlo has learned his lesson. He now tells others to be more careful.
"_____ of scams on the Internet!" he says.
         7

**2 Use the words in the chart to scan the article "Online Job Searches: Beware of
Scammers!" on page 36 of the *Transitions* Student's Book. Complete the chart.**

Things scammers do	Things you should do
1. Scammers *place false ads online to cheat inexperienced job applicants.*	1. Be *cautious!*
2. Scammers	2. Be
3. Scammers	3. Do
	4. Be

Lesson D Reading

1 **Use a dictionary. Fill in the chart with the missing word forms. Then circle the correct words in the sentences below.**

-able   -ance   -ful   -less   -tion

Base form	Noun		Base form	Adjective
1. accept	*acceptance*		5. accept	
2. apply			6. apply	
3. educate			7. care	
4. reflect			8. truth	

9. If you get a good **educated** / **(education)** you will have a better chance of getting a good job.

10. Jim was **careful** / **careless** on his school registration form, so he was asked to fill it out again.

11. The way you fill out your job **applied** / **application** is a **reflection** / **reflected** on yourself.

12. Rebecca was thrilled to get a letter of **accepted** / **acceptance** from the school.

13. It is important to be **truth** / **truthful** on your résumé.

14. Nita's letters of recommendation were not **acceptance** / **acceptable** because they were written by members of her family.

15. If a question doesn't apply to you on a questionnaire, you can write "not **application** / **applicable**."

2 **Look at the article "Ten Tips for a Great Job Application" on page 38 of the *Transitions* Student's Book. Skim the article to answer the questions.**

1. What are acceptable reasons for gaps in employment? _____

   _____

2. What are two reasons for being honest on an application form?

   a. _____

   b. _____

3. How should you answer a question that doesn't apply to you? Why? _____

   _____

4. Why should you write "open" when an application asks about "salary required"? _____

   _____

Lesson E Writing

1 **Read the ad from a university website. Answer the questions.**

New Mesage

Computer Lab Assistants Needed!

Do you have technical skills? Are you looking for part-time work?

The College of Humanities at Miami University is looking for assistants to help in the computer labs during the 2017-2018 academic year. Responsibilities include helping students sign up for and use the computers in the labs; fixing minor computer problems when they occur; and cleaning and locking up the labs at night. Good computer and people skills are required for this job. Interested? Email your résumé and a letter of interest to Mark Bryant, Head of Instructional Computing: mb@cup.org.

1. What skills are needed for this job? _____

2. What are the responsibilities of the job? _____

   _____

3. How do you apply for this job? _____

4. Do you have the skills for this job? Would you be interested in this job? _____

   _____

2 **Look at the cover letter on page 40 of the *Transitions* Student's Book. Write an email version of a cover letter for the job advertised above.**

From:	
To:	Mark Bryant <mb@cup.org>
Date:	
Subject:	Computer lab assistant position

_____

_____

_____

_____

_____

_____

Sincerely,

_____

UNIT 5 SUCCESSFUL INTERVIEWS

Lesson A Listening

1 **Read the sentence starters. Listen to the lecture and take notes. Complete the sentences with your own words.**

1. In North American culture, it's important to be on time because *you don't want to be rude*.

2. Smiling is important because _____.

3. Paying attention to your body language is important because _____
_____.

4. Do your best to remember the other person's name because _____
_____.

5. Never answer your cell phone during an introduction because _____
_____.

2 **Listen to the lecture again. Listen for these excerpts and write the missing words.**

. . . Rule number one in North American culture is – ___*be*___ ___*on*___ ___*time*___.
$\overline{\text{1}}$

If your job interview is set for 9:00 a.m., _____ to get _____ _____,
$\overline{\text{2}}$

at _____. If someone invites you for dinner at 7 o'clock, it's OK to arrive at 7:15; but any

later than that and your host might think you are rude – and that's not the way _____ _____
$\overline{\text{3}}$

a good _____ _____.

Rule number two, and again I'm talking about American culture, is smile! A smile makes you

seem warm and open, and research even shows _____ can _____ _____ _____
$\overline{\text{4}}$

and your mood. . . .

My third rule is – _____ _____ to your _____ _____. Stand up
$\overline{\text{5}}$

straight, make eye contact, and greet your _____ _____ with a _____
$\overline{\text{6}}$

_____. These behaviors will make you seem confident and attractive, and they will

_____ _____ _____ for people _____ _____ you.
$\overline{\text{7}}$

Rule number four is – learn people's names. If it's hard for you to pronounce a name, it's OK

_____ _____ the person _____ _____ _____. And then, do your best to use the
$\overline{\text{8}}$

person's name during your first conversation. . . .

And finally, _____ all your _____ _____ _____ _____ you're meeting. . . .
$\overline{\text{9}}$

Remember, the person in front of you is _____ _____ _____ than _____
$\overline{\text{10}}$

_____ calling you on the phone . . .

Lesson B Past modals

Study the grammar explanation on page 44 of the *Transitions* Student's Book.

1 **Complete the paragraph with the correct past modal form of the verbs.**

Su moved from China to the United States last year. When she first got here, she had a hard time making friends. There are many things she ___*could have done*___ (could / do) to make her transition easier. Su never looked at people when they spoke to her; she _____ (could / make) eye contact with them. Su also frowned when people spoke to her because she couldn't understand them easily; she _____ (should not / frown) because she appeared to be angry. Su was too shy to speak English in her ESL class even though she had learned a lot of English in China; she _____ (should / speak) English with the students in her class. One time, Su's cell phone rang in class. She answered it and the teacher looked very upset; Su _____ (should / tell) her family not to call her during class. Because she was very shy, Su usually walked with her head down; she _____ (should not / walk) with her head down. She _____ (should / look up and smile) at the people around her; she _____ (could / use) body language to show people that she was interested in meeting them. Su has learned a lot since coming to the United States. She is much happier now.

2 **Darab was just fired from his job. Complete the sentences with past modals.**

1. Darab was rude to his co-workers.
   ___*Darab shouldn't have been*___ rude to his co-workers.

2. He didn't make an effort to get to know his co-workers.
   _____ an effort to get to know his co-workers.

3. He never met his deadlines.
   _____ his deadlines.

4. He didn't answer emails from his boss.
   _____ emails from his boss.

5. He took a lot of breaks.
   _____ so many breaks.

6. He often called in sick.
   _____ sick so often.

Lesson C Reading

1 **Write the prefixes. Then complete the sentences with the words. Change the verb form if necessary.**

in-   mis-   un-

1. ___in___ appropriate (adj.)
2. _____ trust (n.)
3. _____ acceptable (adj.)
4. _____ adequate (adj.)
5. _____ motivated (adj.)
6. _____ treat (v.)

7. There was an _____ amount of milk in the fridge. We didn't have enough.

8. That movie is _____ for young children. They shouldn't watch it.

9. The dog was _____ by its former owners and now it is afraid of people.

10. There was so much _____ at my last job that nobody talked to each other.

11. The students were _____. They wanted to play video games instead of studying for the test.

12. The teacher said that it was _____ to turn in homework late.

2 **Complete the chart about the article "Keys to a Successful Interview" on page 46 of the *Transitions* Student's Book. Then scan the article to check your answers.**

Dos and Don'ts for Interviews	
Dos	**Don'ts**
1. Prepare the ___materials___ you need ahead of time.	1. Wear _____ clothing.
2. Arrive _____.	2. Ask about the _____ right away.
3. Learn the _____ of the person who is interviewing you.	3. Be overly _____.
4. Learn something about the _____.	4. Speak _____ about others.
5. Be _____ about your skills, education, and experience.	5. Chew _____ or smell like _____.
6. Be _____ and interested.	6. Act _____ for the position.
7. Follow up with a _____ note.	

Lesson D Reading

1 **Complete the sentences about Farad's job search.**

annoyance	considered	follow up	✓persuade
attitude	favorably	improve	realization

Farad is a student at the community college in his city. He had an interview yesterday for a part-time job as an office assistant at the college. He really wanted the job. At the interview, he had to _____persuade_____ the employer that he was the best candidate for the job.

1
In order to _____ his chances of getting the job, Farad brought some excellent

2
letters of recommendation that were written by two of his professors. The letters made the

employer think _____ about Farad because the professors wrote about how

3
responsible he is. The employer was also impressed by Farad's _____ toward work.

4
Farad has a great work ethic and said he would have no trouble balancing both homework and

work hours.

Farad decided to _____ his interview with a thank-you letter. He only wrote

5
one note because he thought more than one might be _____ annoying, and that

6
_____ might hurt his chances of getting the position.

7
His careful preparation for the office job paid off. He got the job! Farad had applied for another

job that he didn't get, but he came to the _____ that it was probably for the best.

8
The other job was off-campus, and he would have spent a lot of time driving to and from work and

school. Farad was happy with the results of his job search.

2 **Look at the article "Make the Most of Your Interview – Follow Up!" on page 48 of the** *Transitions* **Student's Book. Complete the outline.**

1. Main idea *It is important to follow up after an interview by writing a thank-you note.*

   a. Reason 1 _____

   b. Reason 2 _____

2. If the interview went well, _____

3. If the interview did not go well, _____

4. Write only one thank-you note because _____

Lesson E Writing

1 **Read Sandra's interview for a job at the Botanic Gardens. Answer the questions.**

Cindy Hi, my name is Cindy Boyer. I'm the Employee Coordinator here at the Botanic Gardens. You must be Sandra.

Sandra Yes, I'm Sandra Muller. It's very nice to meet you.

Cindy It's nice to meet you, too. So, why are you interested in working at the Botanic Gardens?

Sandra I've always loved working with plants and in gardens. I have a little garden of my own, and I also volunteer at a community garden.

Cindy That's wonderful. The position you applied for involves working in the gift shop, but knowledge of gardening is a plus. Do you have any experience working in a shop?

Sandra Yes, I've worked in an ice-cream shop for the past three summers.

Cindy Do you know how to work a cash register?

Sandra Yes, I worked the cash register at the ice-cream shop.

Cindy Great. This is a part-time position, 12 hours a week. Do you have any questions?

Sandra If I get the job, will I have to work on weekends?

Cindy Yes, you'll be expected to work one weekend every month. Is that all right?

Sandra That's no problem at all.

Cindy Very good. Here's my card. I'll let you know about the position in about a week.

Sandra Thanks so much. It was wonderful to meet you.

1. Where is the job Sandra is applying for? <u>*at the Botanic Gardens*</u>

2. Will she be working in the garden? _____

3. What experience does Sandra have that is related to this job? _____

4. Why does she want to work there? _____

2 **Look at the sample thank-you email on page 50 of the *Transitions* Student's Book. Write a thank-you letter from Sandra to Cindy.**

Sandra Muller
555 East Walnut Street
Everett, WA 98201

Cindy Boyer
Employee Coordinator
Botanic Gardens
Everett, WA 98203

May 27, 2017

_____ :

_____

_____

_____

_____

_____ ,

_____

UNIT 6 SMALL TALK

Lesson A Listening

1 **Read the statements. Listen to the lecture and circle the main idea.**

1. You shouldn't talk about controversial subjects when you first meet someone.
2. The purpose of small talk is to start a conversation by talking about light, neutral topics.
3. "Safe" topics for small talk include sports and the weather.

2 **Listen to the lecture again. Listen for these excerpts and write the missing words.**

. . . what is small talk? Well, it's kind of casual or "light" conversation about neutral or noncontroversial _subjects_ _like_ _the_ _weather_ or _sports_.
                 1
It's the kind of conversation we have with people in places like parties, or standing in line somewhere, or when we're waiting for a class or a business meeting to start.

One purpose of small talk is to "break the ice," which means to start a conversation with another person, _____ a person you don't _____ _____ _____. It's a
        2
polite way to start talking with someone, and often it's a bridge to talking about bigger topics later, when you feel _____ _____ with _____ _____. Another purpose of small
        3
talk is to fill the time before the start of an event like a meeting or a class.

. . . What should you talk about, and which topics should you avoid? "Safe" topics include the weather and sports, as I said; also anything about your _____ _____ or _____
                   4
_____, your family, traveling, or learning English. Movies, music, and entertainment are also good topics.

Inappropriate topics are things that Americans consider to be private, so _____,
                                           5
_____, _____, and _____ – you shouldn't ask questions about those things until you know people very well. You should never ask Americans _____ _____ _____
                                                                                  6
they _____ or what they paid for something. It's also inappropriate to make negative comments about people's bodies, like saying they've gained weight or that they look sick.

Remember, the purpose of small talk is to open up a conversation and to get to know another person. Don't start out by talking about _____ that are _____ _____ or _____
                                                          7
_____. If you approach another person with respect, and you are careful about the subjects you choose to speak about, people will usually feel comfortable around you. It's also _____
                                                                                     8
_____ _____ to practice _____ _____!

Lesson B Tag questions

Study the grammar explanation on page 54 of the *Transitions* Student's Book.

1 **Read the sentences. Circle the correct tag question.**

1. It's cold today, **is it** / **isn't it?**
2. You haven't met each other yet, **have you** / **haven't you**?
3. She's a great teacher, **is she** / **isn't she**?
4. You didn't finish the book, **did you** / **didn't you**?
5. You don't want to drop the class, **do you** / **don't you**?
6. She hadn't seen the movie before, **had she** / **hadn't she**?
7. That was a hard exam, **was it** / **wasn't it**?
8. That's a great movie, **is it** / **isn't it**?
9. We shouldn't smoke here, **should we** / **shouldn't we**?

2 **Complete the sentences. Make tag questions and answers.**

1. **A** You just arrived in the United States, _____ *didn't you* _____?

   B _____ *Yes, I did* _____. I came here from Mexico yesterday.

2. **A** You've read this book before, _____?

   B _____. I read it last summer

3. **A** You didn't take the American Literature class last year, _____?

   B _____. I'm going to take it in the fall.

4. **A** He's a funny actor, _____?

   B _____. I've seen all his movies.

5. **A** It's hot in here, _____?

   B _____. I'd like a cold drink.

6. **A** You're from Oregon, _____?

   B _____. I'm from Washington.

7. **A** You don't speak Spanish, _____?

   B _____. I learned it in the Peace Corps.

8. **A** You can't come to the museum with us, _____?

   B _____. I have an interview.

9. **A** They should study more, _____?

   B _____. They are very busy though.

Lesson C Reading

1 **Complete the paragraph.**

behavior	polite	✓scenarios	unaware
intention	recognize	specific	wondered

It's very interesting to visit another country and learn about a new culture. Sometimes, however, there are certain situations, or _____scenarios_____ where we can get confused because
₁
of cultural differences. A teacher I know got a job in another country. She tried very hard to

_____ cultural differences in the new country. But it wasn't easy. One day she noticed
₂
that one of her students was wearing new shoes. She complimented the student on the shoes. Her

_____ was to make the girl feel good about her new shoes. The next day the student
₃
brought the teacher the exact pair of shoes in the teacher's size! The teacher was surprised and

_____ why the student had done that. The teacher asked other people from the
₄
host culture about her student's _____. The people she spoke to said that, in their
₅
culture, if you compliment someone on something, it is considered _____ to give the
₆
object mentioned to the person who complimented it. The teacher felt terrible because she was

_____ of the effect that her compliment would have on the student. She thanked the
₇
student and explained the cultural difference to her. In the United States, complimenting someone

is a form of small talk. By complimenting someone on a _____ item they are wearing,
₈
you can begin a conversation.

2 **Scan the article "Small Talk, Big Problems" on page 56 of the *Transitions* Student's Book for the greetings that fit the responses in the chart and for the behaviors that show a speaker is interested. Complete the chart.**

	Greetings	Responses
Openers	1. How are you doing?	Fine, thanks.
	2.	Hello.
	3.	
Closers	4. It was nice to meet you.	You, too.
	5.	Sounds good!
	6.	Great! Talk to you later!

Behaviors that show the speaker is truly interested:

7. makes _____   9. makes an _____

8. waits to _____

Lesson D Reading

1 **Complete the sentences. Use the correct preposition for each phrasal verb. Then match the phrasal verbs with the definitions.**

> in   on   up

1. Lisa wants to fit __in__ when she's in a different country, so she tries to learn about the local culture and customs.

2. After Jana's interview, she followed _____ with a thank-you note.

3. Sarah was working so much that it cut _____ to her study time.

4. Jim is interested in starting _____ his own business.

5. Nabil wants to focus _____ his studies this semester so that he can graduate in June.

6. My new job requires that I call _____ all my knowledge and skills.

__b__ 7. fit __in__	a. recall, draw on	
_____ 8. follow _____	b. belong	
_____ 9. cut _____	c. concentrate on	
_____ 10. start _____	d. do something right after as a next step	
_____ 11. focus _____	e. take away from	
_____ 12. call _____	f. start from the beginning	

2 **Look at the article "Strategies for Successful Small Talk" on page 58 of the *Transitions* Student's Book. Complete the chart below by underlining the key words in each strategy and then scanning the article to find examples of the strategies.**

Strategy	Examples
1. <u>Don't be shy</u> – talk to people you've never met before.	Say, "Nice day, isn't it?
2. Tell funny stories or experiences you've had.	
3. Practice making listening sounds.	
4. Learn to interrupt politely.	
5. Use positive body language.	
6. Learn phrases for exiting conversations gracefully.	
7. Prepare a list of neutral conversation starters.	

Lesson E Writing

1 Look at the diagram about Lee. Read the paragraph and underline the topic sentence and the concluding sentence in the paragraph. Put a check before each supporting sentence.

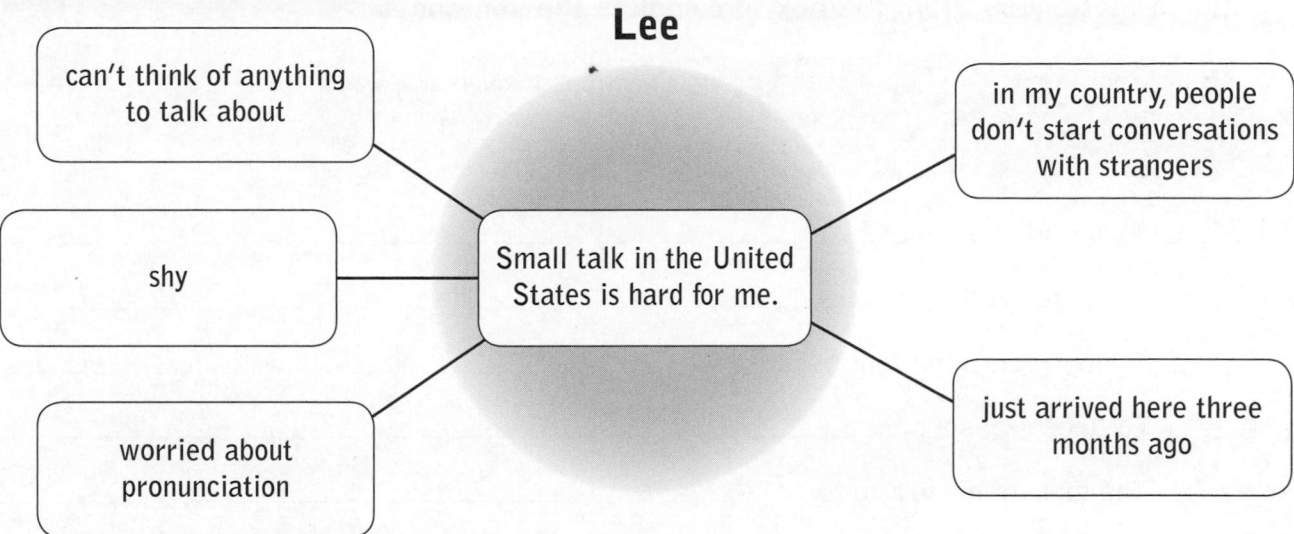

Lee

- can't think of anything to talk about
- shy
- worried about pronunciation
- Small talk in the United States is hard for me.
- in my country, people don't start conversations with strangers
- just arrived here three months ago

Making small talk in the United States is hard for Lee. ✓He is shy, and he feels like he can't think of anything to talk about. He just arrived here three months ago. In his country, people don't start conversations with people they have just met in the supermarket, for example. Lee is also worried about his pronunciation. For all these reasons, his first three months in the United States have been very difficult.

2 Complete a diagram about yourself. Then write a paragraph about yourself on a separate piece of paper.

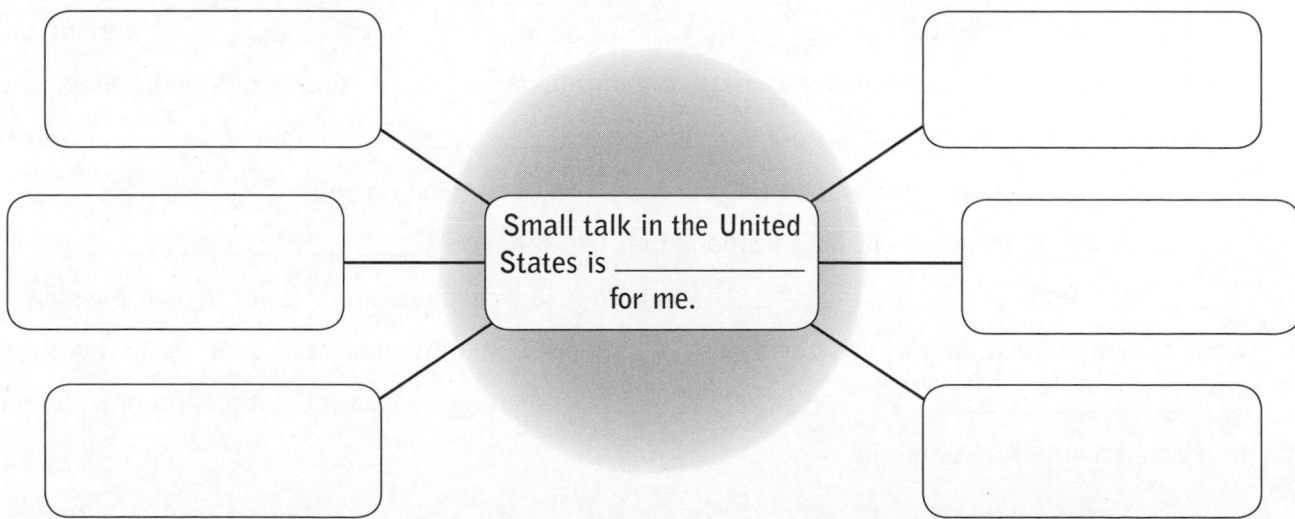

Small talk in the United States is _____ for me.

UNIT 7 IMPROVING RELATIONSHIPS

Lesson A Listening

1 Listen to the lecture and put the transitional phrases in order. Then choose the correct ending from the box to complete the sentences.

> a definition   it makes it easier to accomplish goals
> important benefits, too   teamwork is an essential part of today's society
> ✓ is teamwork

_____ Teamwork has other _____.

_____ Let's start with _____.

_____ Teamwork is important because _____.

_____ For these reasons, _____.

___1___ The topic of my talk today *is teamwork* _____.

2 Listen to the lecture again. Listen for these excerpts and write the missing words.

. . . If you've ever had a job interview, chances are that the interviewer asked you what teamwork means to you, or whether you're a team player, right? Well, ___*what*___ ___*is*___ ___*teamwork*___, and why ___*is*___ ___*it*___ ___*important*___?
                 1
. . . these days it means any group of people who collaborate, I mean who _____ and
                                                                              2
_____ _____, to accomplish a common goal . . .

. . . Especially when you have a large project, it's easier and faster to complete the task when you have a team of people _____ _____ _____ and _____ working on
                            3
different pieces of it. So teamwork benefits organizations, but it can also benefit individuals. If you work as a team at your job or school, _____ _____ _____ more _____ in what
                                        4
you are doing because other people on your team are depending on you.

. . . According to research, organizations that use teamwork _____ _____
                                                              5
_____ and _____ _____ and reduced absenteeism – fewer people missing work or school because of stress or illness. Additionally, when people work together in a group,

_____ _____ _____ _____ such as conflict resolution and how to come
      6
to a consensus or agreement.

Lesson B Unreal conditionals

Study the grammar explanation on page 64 of the *Transitions* Student's Book.

1 Circle the correct words. Then rewrite each sentence a different way. Put the second part of the sentence first.

1. We **got** / **would get** more done if we **worked** / would work as a team.
   If we worked as a team, we would get more done .

2. If Lucy **collaborated** / **would collaborate** with us, we **got** / **could get** the job done faster.

   _____ .

3. If my boss **were** / **would be** more flexible, I **got** / **could get** more work done by working on the weekends.

   _____ .

4. I **learned** / **could learn** a lot if my boss **allowed** / **would allow** me to go to the conference.

   _____ .

5. If I **were** / **would be** you, I **asked** / **would ask** for more time to meet the deadline.

   _____ .

6. We **would have** / **had** more ideas for this project if Michelle **were** / **would be** here.

   _____ .

2 Complete the sentences. Use the present unreal conditional.

1. Miguel likes to work independently.

   If Miguel _____ (work) with a team, he _____ (advance) more quickly.

2. Renee is late to work a lot.

   Renee _____ (not be) late to work so often if her car _____ (work) better.

3. Pete doesn't get along with his co-workers.

   If Pete _____ (work) as part of a team, he _____ (get along) better with his co-workers.

4. The team can't come to a consensus.

   The team _____ (be able) to agree if Pete _____ (not be) so difficult.

Lesson C Reading

1 Scan the article "Bad Behavior in the Workplace" on page 66 of the *Transitions* Student's Book to find different forms of these words. Write the correct word forms in the chart. Use your dictionary to help you.

Nouns	Verbs	Adjectives
1.	enforce	8.
2.	satisfy	9.
3.	bother	10. *bothersome*
4.	harass	11.
5.	use	12.
6.	abuse	13.
7.	bully	14.

2 Look again at the article "Bad Behavior in the Workplace" on page 66 of the *Transitions* Student's Book. Write *F* for fact or *O* for opinion, based on the reading. Facts are pieces of information that are known or have been proven. Opinions are feelings or beliefs.

_F_ 1. According to the Randstad USA survey, the number one pet peeve about workplace behavior is gossiping.

_O_ 2. It is annoying when people waste company time with poor time-management skills.

_____ 3. Bullying and sexual harassment are examples of problems in the workplace.

_____ 4. Both males and females can be victims of sexual harassment.

_____ 5. The use of cell phones in the office is bothersome.

_____ 6. My co-worker's perfume is too strong.

_____ 7. Bullying and sexual harassment are against the law.

_____ 8. People shouldn't leave messes in the lunchroom.

_____ 9. Work rules should be enforced.

_____ 10. A professor who ridicules his student's religious beliefs could be guilty of bullying.

_____ 11. Gossiping is a harmless behavior.

_____ 12. Government offices have written policies that define and prohibit bullying and sexual harassment.

Lesson D Reading

1 **Complete the conversations. You will not use three of the words in the box.**

accusatory	backfired	confrontation	critical	grates
annoying	✓blamed	constructive	diplomacy	sufficient

1. **A** Can you believe that the boss _____*blamed*_____ me for the mess in the lunchroom?

   B I know! He said it was your fault, and it wasn't!

2. **A** My co-worker's habit of talking to her friends on her cell phone all day really _____ on my nerves.

   B How can you stand listening to that all day long?

3. **A** I tried to talk to James about the argument we had yesterday, but it really _____.

   B What do you mean?

   A He got even angrier than he was yesterday. He was yelling at me!

4. **A** I had a meeting with my boss today. She was very _____ of my work habits.

   B Why was she so negative? What did she say?

5. **A** You did a great job talking to your employee about her mistake. You weren't at all _____ or critical.

   B Thanks. I was trying to use the _____ skills we learned in the workshop last week.

6. **A** What is _____ criticism?

   B It means that you give someone ideas for how to improve what they are doing instead of only telling them what they are doing wrong.

2 **Look at the article "Don't Let Annoying People Drive You Nuts" on page 68 of the *Transitions* Student's Book. Complete the chart.**

Reactions	Results (Effects)
get angry	1. *puts you in a bad mood*
	2.
	3.
turn a blind eye	4.
think of the other's feelings	5.
use "I" language	6.
	7.

Lesson E Writing

1 **Read the paragraph about two roommates. Underline the words that show contrast – *but*, *however*, and *on the other hand*. Then complete the notes.**

David and Andrew share a dorm room at their university, <u>but</u> they are very different from each other. David is quiet and studious; he studies all the time. Andrew, however, is the complete opposite. He is very loud and outgoing; he often has his friends over, and he loves to go to parties with them. David always goes to bed early. He has a healthy lifestyle. He tries to get eight hours of sleep each night and he likes to eat healthy food. Andrew, on the other hand, stays up late almost every night and likes to eat junk food. Another problem the roommates have is that they have different tastes in music. David listens only to country music. Andrew hates country music but loves rock music.

David

quiet and studious

2. _____

goes to bed early

4. _____

listens only to country music

Andrew

1. _____

often has his friends over; loves to go to parties

3. _____

likes to eat junk food

5. _____

2 **David wants advice on how to live with Andrew. Look at the letter asking Brenda for advice on page 70 of the *Transitions* Student's Book. Write a letter from David to Brenda. Use words that show contrast.**

_____ ,

_____

_____

_____

_____

_____

_____

3 **Plan a response to David from Brenda. Brainstorm solutions to the problems. Then write your response on a separate piece of paper.**

Solution 1: _____

Solution 2: _____

Solution 3: _____

UNIT 8 GIVING AND RECEIVING CRITICISM

Lesson A Listening

1 **Read the parts of the lecture. Listen to the lecture and number the parts in the order that you hear them. Then complete the chart.**

Parts of the lecture	Main idea of each part
_____ constructive criticism	
__1__ topic	how to give criticism that's fair and constructive
_____ conclusion	
_____ results of negative criticism	
_____ an example of negative criticism	

2 **Listen to the lecture again. Listen for these excerpts and write the missing words.**

. . . Last week Ray had an important exam. . . . when he got his exam back the first thing he saw was a big red F at the top of his paper. The professor . . . had written " _Disappointing_ performance – ___See___ __me__ __in__ my ___office___ " at the bottom

¹

of the paper.

. . . Ray went to see his professor and tried to explain his situation, _____ _____ _____

2

wasn't _____. "You need to try harder," he said. "If you can't handle working and studying at the same time, maybe you should think about quitting school."

This made Ray so angry that he _____ _____ door _____ _____ _____ out of his

3

professor's office. But then he started to think that maybe his professor was right. And three weeks later he dropped out of school.

. . . We see that negative criticism _____ _____ terrible _____. . . . If you

4

have to criticize someone, experts say, _____ _____ constructively, _____ _____.

5

Constructive criticism has three steps: First, say something good about the person or their work. This will help them relax and prepare them for the next step. In step two, _____ _____

6

_____ _____ about _____ _____. Be honest, but be gentle. And don't stop there – talk to the person about solutions to the problem. The goal is to help a person learn and grow,

_____ _____ _____ _____ embarrass _____. Finally, in the third step, _____

7   8

another _____ _____ about the person that lets them know you care about them. This will leave the person feeling _____ instead _____ _____.

9

Lesson B Conditional clauses

Study the grammar explanation on page 74 of the *Transitions* Student's Book.

1 Circle the correct form of the verbs.

1. If Jaime's co-worker **hadn't / haven't** yelled at him, he **wouldn't have been / weren't** so upset.

2. Miranda **would have / will have** gotten a promotion if she **had / would have** received a good annual review at work.

3. Bianca **would have gotten / got** a better grade if she **has / had** studied for the test.

4. If Isabella **had / have** received constructive criticism, she **would have felt / felt** better about the problem.

5. Jeremy **would have / had** gotten promoted if he **had / would have** stayed at his old job.

6. Francisco **would have / had** changed his behavior if he **had / have** known that it was bothering his co-workers.

7. If Ms. Woods **had / have** changed the students' schedules, they **would have / were** been happy.

2 Complete the sentences. Use the past unreal conditional.

1. Raquel got sick. She didn't go to the meeting.

   If Raquel _____*hadn't gotten*_____ (not get) sick, she _____*would have gone*_____ to the meeting.

2. David didn't meet his work deadlines. His co-workers were irritated with him.

   David's co-workers _____ (not be) irritated with him if he

   _____ (meet) his work deadlines.

3. Sasha gave her employees constructive criticism. Her employees listened and changed their work habits.

   If Sasha _____ (not give) her employees constructive criticism, they

   _____ (not listen) and changed their work habits.

4. Ben didn't attend all the study sessions. He didn't pass the exam.

   If Ben _____ (attend) all the study sessions, he _____

   (pass) the exam.

5. The teacher didn't allow the students to turn in their papers via email. They didn't meet the deadline.

   The students _____ (meet) the deadline if their teacher

   _____ (allow) them to turn in their papers via email.

Lesson C Reading

1 Complete the sentences. Four of the words in the box will not be used.

defended	insight	instinctively	rigid	self-righteous	vulnerability
√ defensive	instinct	kernel	rigidly	thoroughly	vulnerable

1. When you are criticized by another person, it's easy to get ___*defensive*___.

2. Some people also act _____, as if they are right and the other person is wrong.

3. It's important not to become _____ when listening to someone who is criticizing you. You should be flexible and consider possible reasons they might be criticizing you.

4. There may be a _____ of truth in what they are saying.

5. Listen to the criticism _____ to see whether or not anything that the other person is saying is correct.

6. If your _____ tells you that the other person is right, then listen carefully to what the person is saying.

7. You may feel _____, as if you could be hurt easily by the criticism.

8. However, if you listen to the other person carefully, you may gain some _____ into the situation. Then you can decide if you agree with the other person or not.

2 Look at the article "Accepting Criticism Gracefully" on page 76 of the *Transitions* Student's Book. Complete the chart. You may need to infer the answer, or use your best judgment based on the information in the article.

Four Steps for Responding Gracefully to Criticism	
What to Do	**What to Say**
1. *Show with a nod that you heard the criticism. Stay calm.*	5. *"I understand how concerned you are about this."*
2.	6.
3.	7.
4.	8.

Lesson D Reading

1 Complete the chart with the correct word forms. Use a dictionary if necessary. Then circle the correct word forms in the sentences.

Nouns	Verbs	Adjectives
1. embarrassment	8. embarrass	15. embarrassed
2.	9.	16. disagreeable
3.	10.	17. weighty
4. surprise	11.	18.
5.	12.	19. prepared
6.	13. calm	20.
7. apology	14.	21.

22. If I had **prepared** / **preparation** more, I would have gotten a better grade on the test.

23. That teacher is so **disagree** / **disagreeable** – I don't like being in his class.

24. I was **surprise** / **surprised** when my co-worker criticized me.

25. How much does that book **weigh** / **weighty**?

26. Jeet looked very **apologize** / **apologetic** after he forgot to email me about the meeting.

27. It was such an **embarrass** / **embarrassment** to forget my interviewer's name!

2 Skim the article "The Performance Evaluation" on page 78 of the *Transitions* Student's Book. Match the sentence parts to give accurate information about the article.

1. John looked rather sad ___c___
2. John lost his cool _____
3. Bill didn't give John a good evaluation _____
4. John didn't really listen _____
5. John reacted to Bill's criticism _____
6. John blamed others _____
7. Serena is a good friend _____
8. At the end of the reading, John _____

a. decided to apologize to Bill.
b. because he felt bad about himself.
c. because he got a bad job evaluation.
d. because she listened to John.
e. when Bill said things he didn't like.
f. because he said John wastes time at work.
g. because he got defensive and started talking about what a good job he does.
h. very defensively.

Lesson E Writing

1 **Read the story. Then answer the questions.**

> Carlos is a manager at a discount store. He oversees the customer service section of the store, supervising the workers who deal with returns and exchanges. Yesterday Carlos noticed the way one of the employees was talking to a customer.
>
> The customer wanted to return a dress. Ted, the employee, quite rudely asked the customer if she had worn the dress and then refused to give the customer back her money because she didn't have a receipt. Ted didn't realize that the store policy was to look up the receipt on the computer by swiping the credit card that the customer had used to purchase the item.
>
> After telling the customer that she could return the dress after all and showing Ted how to look up the receipt, Carlos took Ted aside. He mentioned that he appreciated how dependable Ted was as a worker. Then he pointed out that Ted had been a little short, or rude, with the customer when she brought in the dress to return. Carlos gently told Ted that he should change his manner with the customers a little by being friendlier and more understanding.
>
> Ted took the criticism well – he told Carlos that he would work on being friendlier in the future. Carlos kept an eye on Ted and noticed that he improved his customer service skills after that incident.

1. Who are Carlos and Ted? _____

2. Where did this story take place? _____

3. Why was Ted criticized? _____

4. Was Ted criticized in a constructive way? Why or why not? _____

5. How did Ted respond to the criticism? _____

6. How did Ted's behavior change after Carlos talked to him? _____

2 **Plan a story about a time when you were criticized or you criticized someone else. Answer these questions before writing the story. Then write the story on a separate piece of paper.**

1. Where did the story take place? _____

2. Who were the people in the story? _____

3. Who was criticized? Why? _____

4. Was it constructive criticism? Why or why not? _____

5. How did things change after this incident? _____

UNIT 9 THE RIGHT ATTITUDE

Lesson A Listening

1 **Read the statements. Listen to the lecture and circle the main idea.**

1. Nobody is totally positive or totally negative all the time.
2. Positive people are upbeat and cheerful.
3. A positive attitude helps you have success in your daily life.

2 **Listen to the lecture again. Listen for these excerpts and write the missing words.**

Welcome, everyone, to today's workshop, which we're calling "_Adjusting_ _Your_ (1) _Attitude_ _for_ _Success_." As everybody knows, attitude affects all aspects of our lives – the people around us, the success of our work, and the _enjoyment_ (2) of _our_ _daily_ _tasks_. Whether you think you have a positive or a negative attitude, this class will help you to become more successful at work, at school, and at home. OK?

To begin, how do you recognize a positive person? Well, behavior can reveal a lot about a person's attitude. _Positive_ (3) _people_ are _generally_ _upbeat_ and cheerful. . . . They have a "can-do" attitude, meaning they welcome challenges and believe that there's _a_ (4) _solution_ to _every_ _problem_. Positive people also support their teammates or co-workers. They like to shine a light on other people's accomplishments, and they rarely complain. In short, positive people are _a_ (5) _pleasure_ to _be_ _around_.

Now let's look at the opposite type of person, the person nobody wants to have on their team because of their negative attitude. How do they behave? Well, typically, _negative_ (6) _people_ don't _smile_ _or_ _laugh_ very much, and they always seem to be unhappy about something. . . . They complain that no one wants to eat lunch with them, but they can't see that it's their own negativity that is pushing friends, family, and colleagues away. _Do_ (7) _you_ know _anybody_ _like_ _that_?

Now these are extreme descriptions, of course. _Nobody_ (8) is _totally_ _positive_ or _totally_ _negative_ all the time. But if you feel there's too much negativity in your life and you'd like to take steps to fix it, this class will give you the skills you need to _adjust_ (9) _your_ _attitude_ for a better and _more_ (10) _successful_ _life_. . . .

Lesson B Adverb clauses of concession

Study the grammar explanation on page 84 of the *Transitions* Student's Book.

1 **Combine the two sentences into one new sentence. Use the words in parentheses. Write the new sentence two different ways.**

1. Jeffrey doesn't like his job. Jeffrey makes a lot of money. (even though)

   Even though Jeffrey makes a lot of money, he doesn't like his job.

   Jeffrey doesn't like his job even though he makes a lot of money.

2. Sally has a difficult life. Sally remains positive about the future. (although)

3. Jackson has a lot of friends. Jackson sometimes feels depressed. (even though)

4. Shirley doesn't like it when people criticize her. Shirley criticizes people a lot. (although)

5. Rajiv attended the motivational speaker's lecture. Rajiv didn't feel inspired. (even though)

2 **Make sentences about yourself and other people in your English class.**

1. Although I am very busy, _____.

2. Even though English grammar is difficult, _____.

3. _____ even though my teacher _____.

4. Although my classmates _____.

5. Although living in another country can be hard sometimes, _____.

6. _____ (name of another student in your class) is happy here

   although _____.

Lesson C Reading

1 Below are different forms of several words from the reading "The Power of Positive Thinking" on page 86 of the *Transitions* Student's Book. Look at the article and underline related forms that you find. Then complete the chart. Use a dictionary to help you.

Nouns	Verbs	Adjectives
1. *idyll*	9. *NA*	17. idyllic
2. invasion	10.	18.
3.	11. challenge	19.
4.	12.	20. discouraged
5. determination	13.	21.
6.	14. support	22.
7.	15.	23. adorable
8. interaction	16.	24.

2 Look at the article again. Scan the article for time words and phrases, such as "12 years ago." Underline the time words and phrases. Then fill in the timeline.

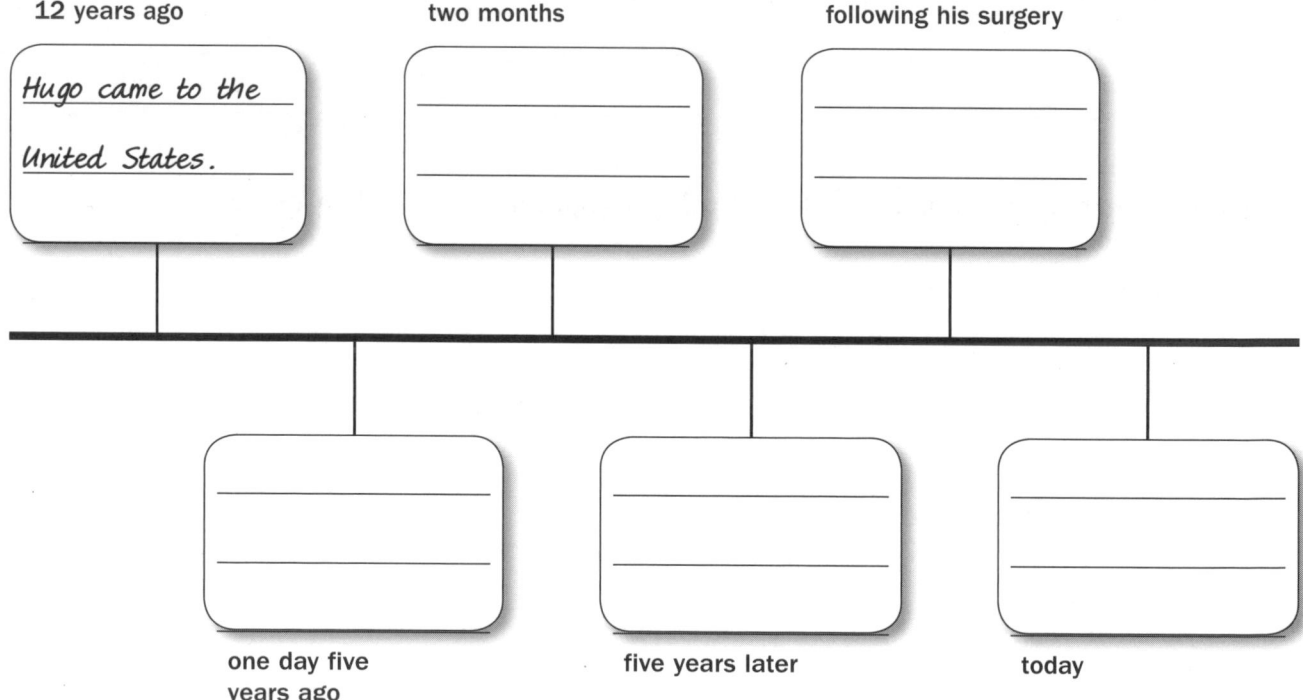

12 years ago

Hugo came to the United States.

two months

following his surgery

one day five years ago

five years later

today

Lesson D Reading

1 Underline the vocabulary words below in the article "Say No to Negativitis" on page 88 of the *Transitions* Student's Book. Find each word in a dictionary. Write the part of speech and the definition that best fits each word in the article.

Vocabulary words	Parts of speech	Definitions
1. gloomy	9. *adjective*	17.
2. contaminate	10.	18.
3. infected	11.	19.
4. absenteeism	12.	20.
5. theft	13.	21.
6. eradicate	14.	22.
7. combat	15.	23.
8. toxic	16.	24.

2 Look again at the article "Say No to Negativitis." Skim the article for information about the topics in the chart. Complete the chart with the topic sentences.

Topics	Topic sentences
example of a person with a negative attitude	1. *Meet Nelly.*
negativitis	2.
causes	3.
effects	4.
role of employee	5.

Lesson E Writing

1 Kevin wants to study in Costa Rica for a year. He is writing an essay as part of his application to study abroad. Read the essay. Underline the introductory and concluding statements. Then circle each transitional phrase, which introduces each reason.

Essay Question: How does a year of living and studying abroad fit into your overall educational goals?

I am very interested in studying in Costa Rica for several reasons. First of all, I would like to become fluent in Spanish. I already have an intermediate level of Spanish, but I would like to increase my level so that I can communicate easily with native speakers. My goal is to get my teaching certificate in teaching English and to minor in Spanish. If I can speak Spanish fluently, it will help me to teach English to Spanish-speaking students in the future. Secondly, I am very interested in living in and learning about a new culture. This will help me understand what my students are going through. Studying in Costa Rica would allow me to immerse myself in Costa Rican culture. I spent a semester in Madrid during high school. While I was there, I lived with a family and studied Spanish. I had no problems adjusting to living in a new country, so I know that I would also adapt well to living in Costa Rica. My final reason is to get the credits I need to get my minor in Spanish. If I spend a year abroad in Costa Rica, I can take all the courses that I need to fulfill my minor. This will be an enjoyable and educational way for me to enhance my studies. For all of these reasons, studying abroad in Costa Rica for a year definitely fits into my overall educational goals.

---

2 Plan an essay for your professor answering the question: "How does taking this course fit into your overall goals?" Complete the outline. Then write the essay on a separate piece of paper, adding support for each of your reasons.

Introductory statement: _____

Transition Word + Reason 1: _____

_____

Transition Word + Reason 2: _____

_____

Transition Word + Reason 3: _____

_____

Concluding statement: _____

Lesson A Listening

1 Listen to the lecture and circle the types of writing that you hear.

business reports   (daily progress reports)   restaurant orders

compositions   essays   shopping lists

computer reports   math reports   work orders

2 Listen to the lecture again. Listen for these excerpts and write the missing words.

Today I want to talk to you about the importance of writing. No matter ___what___ [1] ___your___ future job ___is___, chances are you will have to do some kind of writing. For example, nursing assistants have to ___write___ [2] ___daily___ progress ___reports___ on their patients. Automotive technicians need to write work orders for cars that need repairs. Housekeepers have to write shopping lists.

To show just how important writing is, let me quote you some of the findings ___from___ [3] a ___2,10___ ___reports___ by the National Commission on Writing for America's Families, Schools and Colleges. Number one: Two-thirds, that's more than 60 percent, of salaried workers in large American companies – ___that___ [4] means ___full___, ___time___ ___career workers___ – have to do some kind of writing in their jobs. Number two: . . . Number three: Moving into the future, job seekers who cannot write well will ___problably___ [5] not ___get___ ___hired___, and workers who already have jobs may not get promoted if they don't have good writing skills. Number four: Good writing skills are so important that the Commission found that companies spend up to three billion dollars a year on improving their workers' writing skills ___to___ [6] ___make___ ___them___ more ___productions___

The Commission's conclusion was that in today's job market, writing skills are just as important as math and computer skills. Furthermore, if you learn to write well in school, it ___would___ [7] ___transfer___ to ___almost___ any ___job___, from taking orders in a restaurant to writing business reports for a company. . . .

So if you want to improve your writing skills, take classes and practice writing as much as possible. And have patience. It takes time to learn how to write well, but if you practice regularly, you can learn how to write ___more___ [8] ___clearly___, accurately, and ___consciously___.

Lesson B Causative verbs

Study the grammar explanation on page 94 of the *Transitions* Student's Book.

1 Write causative sentences about Rachel's busy week last week. Use the words provided with either *have*, *get*, or *make*.

1. Rachel / her students / write an essay about their career goals

   Rachel had her students write an essay about their career goals.

2. Rachel / her children / clean up their bedrooms before their grandmother came over

   _____

3. Rachel's neighbor / Rachel / bring a potluck dish to her party

   _____

4. Rachel / her husband / to go to the opera with her

   _____

5. Rachel / her daughter / practice piano / every day / even though she didn't want to

   _____

2 Read the paragraph. Underline the eight things students did wrong when their teacher was gone. Then write sentences to describe what the teacher did when she returned. Use the causative verbs *have*, *get*, and *make*.

> The ninth grade students at Belleview High School had a substitute teacher all last week. Their regular teacher was at a conference. The substitute teacher was not very strict, so many students misbehaved. First of all, the students didn't do any work at all. They didn't start the project the teacher had assigned them before she went to the conference. They threw their trash on the floor, and they rearranged the desks. Furthermore, they talked and texted on their cell phones; they didn't listen to the substitute at all. They even used the computers to watch TV shows. When their regular teacher came back, she had a lot of work to do!

rigorous severe [handwritten margin note]

1. (have) *She had the students do some work.*
2. (get) *She got the students do the project.*
3. (have) *She had the students pick up their trash, and arranged the desks.*
4. (make) *She made the students leave your cell phones at home.*
5. (have) *She had the students*
6. (make) _____
7. (get) _____

Lesson C Reading

1 **Complete the sentences. Four of the words in the box will not be used.**

attachment	essential	innovative	savvy	tweeting
electronic	etiquette	lowercase	seminar	vague

1. Nolan's answer was so _____ vague _____ that I couldn't figure out what he was talking about.

2. I wish I were more _____ savvy (experien te) _____ about computers – when something goes wrong, I can never figure out what the problem is.

3. Did you go to the _____ seminar _____ on how to be a more positive person? I wanted to go, but I missed it.

4. If you want to do well in a job interview, it is absolutely _____ essential _____ that you portray yourself as a positive person.

5. Did you get the email _____ attachment _____? It had information about the meeting in it.

6. It is good _____ etiquette _____ to respond to an invitation to say if you will attend or not. This helps the host or hostess plan for refreshments.

Leia o artigo

2 **Read Robin's email. Skim the article "Email Etiquette 101" on page 96 of the _Transitions_ Student's Book, and write five problems with her messaget.**

⚪⚪⚪	New Message
From:	Robin Hill
Subject:	stuff 📎
Date:	June 3, 2017
To:	Dr. Samuel Gardener, Rita Smith, John Jacobs, Ritchie Garcia, Sarah Hall

hey sam,

I didn't go to the meeting because I was sooooo busy. I know that you're the boss so I should have gone to the meeting, but I couldn't because of a bunch of stuff, so I hope you won't fire me – lol. I'm sending this to the whole office so everyone knows why I didn't go. Hey I'm also attaching the work file you wanted. It's kinda big so watch out! I also forwarded your last email about the problems in the office to a bunch of other people.

See ya tomorrow,
Robin

1. _The subject is vague._

2. _started the email with lowercase_

3. _used informal language._

4. _Forwarded the email to the whole officce._

5. _____

Lesson D Reading

1 **Circle the correct words.**

1. If someone beats around the bush, it means they **get** / **(don't get)** to the point right away.

2. Since Jim skimmed the article, he **read** / **didn't read** it thoroughly.

3. It was a pleasure to read her essay because her words flowed smoothly; it was **easy** / **not easy** to read.

4. The teacher said that the book is required reading – you **have to** / **don't have to** read it.

5. *First and foremost* means that the item is the **most** / **least** important.

6. The headline grabbed my attention – I wanted to read the article **immediately** / **after a little while**.

7. If your writing is crisp and concise, it is very **clear** / **unclear** and to the point.

8. Ted read the article in depth – he **skimmed** / **didn't skim** it.

2 **Read the problems in the chart. Complete the chart with possible consequences and suggestions for solving the problems in the article "Good Business Writing Doesn't Beat Around the Bush" on page 98 of the *Transitions* Student's Book.**

Problems	Consequences	Suggestions
1. Someone writes a business letter. It is three pages long, with no paragraphs. The letter is full of technical terms that most people don't understand.	4. *It causes confusion for the reader who may not have time to read it in depth.*	7.
2. You receive an action plan at work. It contains the sentences "Employees will be notified when there is a change in plans" and "Your claims will be checked by our business office."	5.	8.
3. The boss of a company reads a letter of recommendation about a potential employee. The letter describes the employee as being "a very nice, good person who does great things and has great experience."	6.	9.

Lesson E Writing

1 **Read the action plan. Complete the chart.**

We are experiencing a problem in the lunchroom. All employees are allowed to use the refrigerator to store their lunch and snacks. However, anyone who uses the refrigerator is also responsible for keeping it clean. Currently, we have the problem that employees are leaving food in the refrigerator and forgetting about it. The food rots and begins to smell. No one volunteers to clean out the refrigerator, and the lunchroom has become smelly and unpleasant. The food is not labeled, so nobody is sure who is leaving it there.

In order to stop this problem and to prevent it from happening in the future, we are implementing the following changes:

1. If you wish to use the refrigerator, please label your food items with your name and the date.

Any unlabeled food will be thrown out at the end of the day.

2. There is a sign-up sheet on the refrigerator. Please sign up to clean it out twice a month. Cleaning it out includes wiping it out with a sponge and dish soap and throwing out unlabeled food. If you do not sign up to clean it out, or if you fail to do so on your designated day, you will lose your privilege to use it.

3. Please respect your colleagues' labeled food items, and do not take them out of the refrigerator. Anyone caught doing so will lose their refrigerator privileges.

This plan will be implemented immediately. Several employees have already volunteered to clean out the refrigerator this week. We thank them for volunteering their time.

Problem	1. *Employees are leaving food in the refrigerator and forgetting about it. The lunchroom is smelly and unpleasant because the food in the refrigerator is rotting.*
Recommendations to correct the problem	2.
Consequences if no action is taken	3.
Timeline	4.

2 **Write an action plan. Choose one of the problems below, or invent your own problem. Complete the chart. Then write your action plan on another piece of paper.**

1. Workers think the new employee work schedule is unfair.

2. A professor assigns too much homework.

3. The library closes early on the weekends; students need a place to study.

Problem	
Recommendations to correct the problem	
Consequences if no action is taken	
Timeline	

ANSWER KEY

Unit 1: Selling yourself

Lesson A: Listening
Exercise 1 page 2
1. F   3. F   5. F
2. T   4. T   6. T

Exercise 2 page 2
1. successful
2. knowledge
3. technician
4. medications
5. operate
6. enthusiastic
7. transferable
8. attitude

Lesson B: Participial adjectives
Exercise 1 page 3
1. exciting   4. relaxing
2. frustrated   5. bored
3. tiring   6. annoyed

Exercise 2 page 3
1. boring   interested
2. excited   tired
3. thrilling   frightening

Lesson C: Reading
Exercise 1 page 4
1. set   4. measure
2. challenging 5. deadline
3. achieve   6. realistic

Exercise 2 page 4
1. b. should be circled
2. a. The goal should be detailed.
   b. It should be measurable.
   c. It should be realistic.
   d. It should have a completion date.

Lesson D: Reading
Exercise 1 page 5
1. committed   6. successful
2. leadership   7. impression
3. communicate   8. recognize
4. maturity   9. analyzing
5. analyze   10. commitment

Exercise 2 page 5
1. Communication skills – get along well with others
2. Leadership skills – think for yourself, make independent decisions
3. Maturity – manage time well, take responsibility for mistakes
4. Problem-solving skills – able to recognize and solve problems
5. Commitment – work hard toward goals
6. Informational skills – able to gather, organize, and analyze information

Lesson E: Writing
Exercise 1 page 6
Objective: Get a job as a patient care technician

Education: Nursing degree, University of Bamako, Mali

High school diploma, International School of Bamako, Mali

Work experience: Red Cross Hospital, Bamako, Mali, 2014–2017

Volunteer Experience: University Medical Center, Tucson, AZ, 2017–present

Skills: Able to take care of sick children; speak French and English; get along with everyone

Unit 2: Building self-confidence

Lesson A: Listening
Exercise 1 page 7
2. is the main idea

Exercise 2 page 7
1. dedicated
2. conscientious
3. optimistic
4. judges
5. criticizes
6. disappointed
7. promotion
8. responsibilities

Lesson B: The present passive
Exercise 1 page 8
1. is judged
2. is affected
3. is pressured
4. are not required
5. are not asked
6. is expected
7. is stressed
8. is influenced

Exercise 2 page 8
1. Students are not allowed to smoke in the buildings.
2. Food or drink is not permitted in the computer lab.
3. A permit is required to park in the parking lot.
4. A fee is charged for students to use the gym.
5. Guest passes are provided to visitors.
6. Students are expected to meet with the counselor.
7. Late students are not admitted into class.
8. Grades are posted on a bulletin board in the hall.

Lesson C: Reading
Exercise 1 page 9
Noun
motivation
criticism
influence
stress
success
encouragement
judgment
product

Verb
motivate
criticize
influence
stress
succeed
encourage
judge
produce

Adjective
motivated, motivational
critical
influential, influenced
stressed, stressful
successful
encouraged, encouraging
judgmental
productive

Exercise 2 page 9
1. understanding self-confidence
2. believing in yourself and your abilities
3. eager, assertive, motivated, willing to accept criticism, emotionally mature, optimistic, productive

4. withdrawn, unmotivated, overly sensitive to criticism, distrustful, pessimistic
5. life experiences with parents, siblings, friends, and teachers
6. a. judging self too harshly
   b. focusing too much on failures
   c. placing pressure on self to succeed
   d. setting unrealistic goals
   e. being fearful of making mistakes

Lesson D: Reading
Exercise 1 page 10
1. *conscientious*
2. assertive
3. loyal
4. reliable
5. creative
6. cooperative
7. *conscientious*
8. creative
9. assertive
10. loyal
11. reliable
12. cooperative

Exercise 2 page 10
1. *How do you build self-confidence?*
2. why people might lack confidence
3. steps to building self-confidence
4. process
5. steps or strategies
6. a. qualities
   b. positively about yourself
   c. realistic goals
   d. successes, failures
   e. assertive
   f. creative outlet

Lesson E: Writing
Exercise 1 page 11
Raymond's strengths: *interested in electronics*, very knowledgeable, motivated, ambitious
Raymond's weaknesses: needs to be a better team player, impatient, gets annoyed easily, not flexible

Unit 3: Volunteering

Lesson A: Listening
Exercise 1 page 12
1. a. *It is a type of on-the-job training.*
   b. You can meet wonderful people and help them.

2. Any four of the following:
   tutor
   help at a day-care center
   help in a nursing home
   build low-cost housing
   remove graffiti
   work at a food bank
3. a. language tutor
   b. help in a health clinic

Exercise 2 page 12
1. *beneficial*
2. training
3. abilities
4. day-care
5. elderly
6. low-cost
7. graffiti
8. food bank

Lesson B: Indirect (reported) speech
Exercise 1 page 13
1. *direct*
2. indirect
3. indirect
4. direct
5. indirect
6. indirect
7. direct

Exercise 2 page 13
(Note: *that* is optional in the following sentences)
1. *Abdul said that he wanted to volunteer at the library.*
2. He said that he was studying to be a librarian.
3. He mentioned that he wanted to get on-the-job training.
4. He added that he was interested in becoming a children's librarian at a public library.
5. Abdul said that he wanted to practice reading stories aloud to children.
6. He said that it was also a good way to improve his English speaking skills.
7. He mentioned that he could put this volunteer experience on his résumé.
8. Abdul told me that he was going to start out by shelving books at the library.
9. Abdul added that he thought it would be a very interesting volunteer position.

Lesson C: Reading
Exercise 1 page 14
1. *coordinator*
2. recruiting
3. supervises
4. popularity
5. recycling
6. collection
7. combine
8. passion
9. committed
10. supports

Exercise 2 page 14
The Venn diagram could include any of the following information:
Sarah:
Community College sophomore
Student Coordinator for Recycling
supervises four volunteers
developed a central recycling site
ordered new collection bins
recruited Audrey as her first volunteer
majoring in environmental studies

Both (overlapping circle):
Sisters
work in recycling program at their community college
committed to recycling

Audrey:
First year at college
wasn't sure she had time for a volunteer job
thought it would be too much work
worked with Sarah/became her sister's first volunteer
wants to make a difference
discovered that volunteering was easier than she thought it would be

Lesson D: Reading
Exercise 1 page 15
1. *are*
2. can
3. is
4. schedule
5. without
6. should
7. are
8. is

Exercise 2 page 15
Topic sentence: *There are many benefits to volunteering while in college.*

Transition 1: *First of all,*
Benefit 1: You can get college credit for volunteering at some schools.
Example 1: Students at Holyoke Community College get college credit for volunteering at community organizations.

Transition 2: A second benefit
Benefit 2: Volunteering can help satisfy college requirements.
Example 2: Students at UC Santa Barbara are required to do 20 hours of community service their last two years

Transition 3: A third benefit
Benefit 3: Looks good on a résumé
Example 3: This can help you get an interview.
Concluding sentence: The most important aspect of community service is making a difference.

Lesson E: Writing
Exercise 1 page 16

1. Introduction: *The Peace Corps is a program that sends volunteers to work in developing countries. Its aim is to help countries with their needs and to help Americans learn about and understand other cultures.*
2. Volunteers: Americans of all ages; education or experience in areas such as language teaching, nursing, engineering, or business; most have at least a bachelor's degree and commit to a two-year term.
3. Benefit for host country: help to improve teaching, health services, conditions of cities, and farming techniques.
4. Benefit for volunteer: learn another language, experience another culture, develop job and leadership skills.
5. Conclusion: Both volunteers and the host countries benefit from the Peace Corps.

Unit 4: Effective job applications

Lesson A: Listening
Exercise 1 page 17

_4_ ask previous employers for references
_5_ you'll need to write a résumé
_1_ deciding what type of job you want
_2_ start looking for jobs in your area
_3_ filling out applications
_6_ you may need to write a cover letter

1. *The first step is / deciding what type of job you want.*
2. Next, / start looking for jobs in your area.
3. The third step is / filling out applications.
4. Fourth, / ask previous employers for references.

5. Next, / you'll need to write a résumé.
6. Finally, / you may need to write a cover letter.

Exercise 2 page 17

1. *What kind of / do you have?*
2. find out
3. word of mouth
4. find applications online
5. don't lie
6. think of / friend / teacher
7. résumé writing / next meeting
8. interested in

Lesson B: Past perfect
Exercise 1 page 18

1. *had prepared*
2. had researched
3. had written (*had* written OK, but *had* is not necessary with *and*)
4. had filled
5. had answered
6. had not/hadn't worked
7. had not/hadn't left
8. had explained
9. had not/hadn't worked
10. had done

Exercise 2 page 18

1. *(1, 2) John had worked for three years as a teacher's assistant* before *he got his teaching certificate.*
2. (2, 1) John had seen many online ads for teachers *when* he decided to apply for a job.
3. (1, 2) *By the time* John finally got an interview, many people had interviewed for the job.
4. (2, 1) John had gotten good letters of recommendation from his previous employers *before* he went to the interview.
5. (2, 1) *After* the principal had read John's wonderful letters of recommendation, he decided to hire him.

Lesson C: Reading
Exercise 1 page 19

1. *inexperienced*
2. applicants
3. scammer
4. realize
5. cautious
6. deception
7. Beware

Exercise 2 page 19
Things scammers do
Answers may include any of the following:
Place false ads online to cheat inexperienced job applicants.
Steal money from bank accounts.
Illegally use credit card numbers.
Use tricks and deception to get private information from people.
Use false Internet job listings to gain people's personal information.

Things you should do

1. Be *cautious!*
2. Be wary of online ads that do not mention the company name or that offer a salary that seems too good to be true.
3. Do some research to see if the company you are dealing with is real.
4. Be careful when you give your personal information to an employer online.

Lesson D: Reading
Exercise 1 page 20

1. *acceptance*
2. application
3. education
4. reflection
5. acceptable
6. applicable
7. careful, careless
8. truthful

9. *education*
10. careless
11. application / reflection
12. acceptance
13. truthful
14. acceptable
15. applicable

Exercise 2 page 20

1. returned to school, moved, volunteered
2. a. This information will become part of your employment history.
   b. You could lose your job if someone finds out that you lied.
3. Write "N/A" or "not applicable." This will show the employer you are careful.
4. This shows a positive attitude toward discussions about your pay.

Lesson E: Writing
Exercise 1 page 21
1. computer and people skills
2. Helping students sign up for and use the computers in the labs; fixing minor computer problems when they occur; and cleaning and locking up the labs at night
3. Email your résumé and a letter of interest to: Mark Bryant, Head of Instructional Computing, mb@cup.org
4. *Answers will vary.*

Exercise 2 page 21
Answer will vary. Possible answer:
From: (name of student)
To: Mark Bryant <mb@cup.org>
Date: (today's date)
Subject: Computer lab assistant position

Dear Mr. Bryant:

I read the advertisement for a computer lab assistant on the university Web site. I am very interested in this position and believe that I have the qualities that you are looking for in a job applicant.

I have always been interested in working with computers and can fix minor computer problems. I also have good organizational and people skills – I have volunteered as an office assistant at my daughter's elementary school for the past three years.

I am enclosing my résumé. I look forward to hearing from you soon.

Sincerely,

(Student's name)

Unit 5: Successful interviews

Lesson A: Listening
Exercise 1 page 22
Answers will vary, but should include at least some of the following ideas:
1. *you don't want to be rude* / you want to make a good impression
2. it makes you seem warm and open, and it can improve your health and mood.

3. it will make you seem confident and attractive, and it will make people remember you.
4. doing this will make you seem polite and truly interested in getting to know the other person.
5. the person in front of you is always more important than the person calling you on the phone.

Exercise 2 page 22
1. *be on time*
2. try / there early / 8:45
3. to make / first impression
4. smiling / improve your health
5. pay attention / body language
6. new acquaintance / firm handshake
7. make it easy / to remember
8. to ask / to repeat it
9. focus / attention on the person
10. always more important / the person

Lesson B: Past modals
Exercise 1 page 23
1. *could have done*
2. could have made
3. should not/shouldn't have frowned
4. should have spoken
5. should have told
6. should not/shouldn't have walked
7. should have looked up and smiled
8. could have used

Exercise 2 page 23
1. *Darab shouldn't have been*
2. He could/should have made
3. He should have met
4. He should have answered
5. He should not/shouldn't have taken
6. He should not/shouldn't have called in

Lesson C: Reading
Exercise 1 page 24
1. *in*appropriate
2. mistrust
3. unacceptable
4. inadequate
5. unmotivated
6. mistreat
7. inadequate
8. inappropriate
9. mistreated
10. mistrust
11. unmotivated
12. unacceptable

Exercise 2 page 24
Dos
1. *materials*
2. early
3. name
4. company, school, or organization beforehand
5. honest
6. positive
7. thank-you

Don'ts
1. inappropriate
2. salary
3. nervous
4. negatively
5. gum / smoke
6. desperate

Lesson D: Reading
Exercise 1 page 25
1. *persuade*
2. improve
3. favorably
4. attitude
5. follow up
6. considered
7. annoyance
8. realization

Exercise 2 page 25
1. *It is important to follow up after an interview by writing a thank-you note.*
   a. You will remind the interviewer that you are truly motivated and interested.
   b. It will show that you have good manners.
2. a thank-you note may persuade the employer to select you over the other competing candidates.
3. the note can help the interviewer remember you favorably even if you are not selected.
4. you do not want to become an annoyance.

Lesson E: Writing
Exercise 1 page 26
1. *at the Botanic Gardens*
2. No, in the gift shop.
3. She has a little garden of her own, she has volunteered at a community garden, and she has experience working the cash register at an ice-cream shop.
4. She has always loved working with plants and in gardens.

Exercise 2 page 26

Answer will vary. Possible answer:

Dear Ms. Boyer:

Thank you very much for inviting me for an interview today at the Botanic Gardens. I enjoyed meeting you very much. I think that my experience working in gardens and working the cash register at an ice-cream shop make me a good candidate for this job. I've always wanted to work in the gift shop at the Botanic Gardens. Working one weekend a month is also not a problem for me.

Thanks again. I look forward to hearing from you soon.

Sincerely,

Sandra Muller

Unit 6: Small talk

Lesson A: Listening
Exercise 1 page 27
#2 should be circled.

Exercise 2 page 27
1. *subjects like the weather / sports*
2. especially / know very well
3. more comfortable / each other
4. native country / your language
5. religion, politics, sex / money
6. how much money / make
7. subjects / too personal / too heavy
8. a great way / your English

Lesson B: Tag questions
Exercise 1 page 28
1. *isn't it*
2. have you
3. isn't she
4. did you
5. do you
6. had she
7. wasn't it
8. isn't it
9. should we

Exercise 2 page 28
1. **A** *didn't you* / **B** *Yes, I did.*
2. **A** haven't you / **B** Yes, I have.
3. **A** did you / **B** No, I didn't.
4. **A** isn't he / **B** Yes, he is.
5. **A** isn't it / **B** Yes, it is.

6. **A** aren't you / **B** No, I'm not.
7. **A** do you / **B** Yes, I do.
8. **A** can you / **B** No, I can't.
9. **A** shouldn't they / **B** Yes, they should.

Lesson C: Reading
Exercise 1 page 29
1. *scenarios*
2. recognize
3. intention
4. wondered
5. behavior
6. polite
7. unaware
8. specific

Exercise 2 page 29
1. *How are you doing?*
2. How are you?
3. Hello.
4. *It was nice to meet you.*
5. I'll call you.
6. Let's talk soon.
7. eye contact
8. hear your answer
9. appointment with you for a specific day and time

Lesson D: Reading
Exercise 1 page 30
1. *in*
2. up
3. in
4. up
5. on
6. up
7. b / fit *in*
8. d / follow up
9. e / cut in
10. f / start up
11. c / focus on
12. a / call up

Exercise 2 page 30
(any of the following can be used as examples):
1. *Say, "Nice day, isn't it?"* (underline don't be shy)
2. (funny stories or experiences) (underline funny)
3. "I see," "Yes, of course," "Uh-huh," "Really," or "Wow!"(underline listening sounds)
4. "Excuse me," "pardon me," "sorry" and then ask a question (underline interrupt politely)
5. Smile, make eye contact, nod (underline body language)
6. "It's been great talking to you, but I really have to go," "It was nice talking to you" (underline exiting conversations gracefully)
7. "Excuse me," "Do you have the time?" "Where's the bus stop?" or "It's not supposed to rain, is it?" (underline neutral conversation starters)

Lesson E: Writing
Exercise 1 page 31
Topic sentence: Making small talk in the United States. is hard for Lee.

Supporting sentences:
He is shy.
He just arrived here three months ago.
In his country, people don't start conversations.
Lee is also worried about his pronunciation.

Concluding sentence: For all of these reasons, his first three months in the United States have been difficult.

Exercise 2 page 31
Diagrams and paragraphs will vary according to student's opinions.

Unit 7: Improving relationships

Lesson A: Listening
Exercise 1 page 32
_4_ important benefits, too
_2_ a definition
_3_ it makes it easier to accomplish goals
_5_ teamwork is an essential part of today's society
_1_ *is teamwork*

Exercise 2 page 32
1. *what is teamwork / is it important*
2. work / think together
3. with different strengths / abilities
4. you will feel / invested
5. have better employee / student involvement
6. they learn valuable skills

Lesson B: Unreal conditionals
Exercise 1 page 33
1. *If we worked as a team, we would get more done.*
2. We could get the job done faster if Lucy collaborated with us.
3. I could get more work done by working on the weekends if my boss were more flexible.
4. If my boss allowed me to go to the conference, I could learn a lot.

5. I would ask for more time to meet the deadline if I were you.
6. If Michelle were here, we would have more ideas for this project.

Exercise 2 page 33
1. worked / would advance
2. wouldn't be / worked
3. worked / would get along
4. would be able / weren't

Lesson C: Reading
Exercise 1 page 34
Nouns
1. enforcement
2. satisfaction
3. bother
4. harassment
5. use
6. abuse
7. bully

Adjectives
8. enforceable
9. satisfied, satisfying
10. *bothersome*
11. harassed
12. useful
13. abusive
14. bullying

Exercise 2 page 34
1. *F*   4. F   7. F   10. F
2. O   5. O   8. O   11. O
3. F   6. O   9. O   12. F

Lesson D: Reading
Exercise 1 page 35
1. *blamed*
2. grates
3. backfired
4. critical
5. accusatory / diplomacy
6. constructive

Exercise 2 page 35
Results (Effects)
1. *puts you in a bad mood*
2. increases your stress level
3. makes you say things that you might regret later
4. you will become resentful
5. the other person will not feel so bad
6. you will be heard more
7. it is more effective

Lesson E: Writing
Exercise 1 page 36
But, *however*, and *on the other hand* should be underlined.
1. very loud and outgoing
2. studies all the time
3. stays up late almost every night
4. likes to eat healthy food
5. loves rock music

Exercise 2 page 36
Possible answer (answers will vary):
Dear Brenda:

I have a problem with my roommate. We have very different tastes and lifestyles. I am a quiet, studious person, but my roommate is loud and likes parties. I like to go to bed early – he goes to bed late. I eat healthy food and lead a healthy lifestyle – on the other hand, he eats junk food and doesn't get a lot of sleep. I prefer country music, however he prefers rock music. If you were me, what would you do?

Can't Stand This Much Longer

Exercise 3 page 36
Possible answer (answers will vary)

Solution 1: Request a different roommate.
Solution 2: Try to talk to your roommate and figure out how to compromise so that both of you can be happy.
Solution 3: Talk to a counselor on campus to try to resolve your differences.

Dear Can't Stand This Much Longer:

It sounds like you have a major problem. If I were you, I would ask the person in charge of your dorm if you can have a different roommate. Explain the problems that you are having with your roommate. If it isn't possible to do this, try to talk to Andrew to see if you can make some compromises. Maybe he can party with his friends in another

place while you study. Use headphones when you listen to music. There are ways that you can live together in peace.

Good luck!

Brenda

Unit 8: Giving and receiving criticism
Lesson A: Listening
Exercise 1 page 37
1. topic: *how to give criticism that's fair and constructive*
2. an example of negative criticism: the case of a student named Ray
3. results of negative criticism: it can make people angry and cause them to lose confidence and motivation
4. constructive criticism: it has three steps
5. conclusion: Ray's professor might have been able to help him

Exercise 2 page 37
1. *Disappointing / See me in / office*
2. but the professor / sympathetic
3. slammed the / on the way
4. can have / consequences
5. do it / or positively
6. talk to the person / their mistakes
7. not to hurt or / them
8. offer / positive statement
9. motivated / of discouraged

Lesson B: Conditional clauses
Exercise 1 page 38
1. hadn't / wouldn't have been
2. would have / had
3. would have gotten / had
4. had / would have felt
5. would have / had
6. would have / had
7. had / would have

Exercise 2 page 38
1. *hadn't gotten / would have gone*
2. wouldn't have been / had met
3. hadn't given / wouldn't have listened
4. had attended / would have passed
5. would have met / had allowed

Lesson C: Reading

Exercise 1 page 39

1. *defensive*
2. self-righteous
3. rigid
4. kernel
5. thoroughly
6. instinct
7. vulnerable
8. insight

Exercise 2 page 39
What to do

1. *Show with a nod that you heard the criticism. Stay calm.*
2. Ask for more information.
3. Both parties should seek to find something they can agree on.
4. Respond to the criticism after asking permission.

What to Say

5. *"I understand how concerned you are about this."*
6. "Can you give me more information?" / "Could you tell me more about that?"
7. "I understand your need to be very thorough" / "If I had known how much you cared about the project . . .
8. "May I give you my opinion?" / "What can we do to make things better?"

Lesson D: Reading

Exercise 1 page 40
Nouns

1. embarrassment
2. disagreement
3. weight
4. surprise
5. preparation
6. calmness, calm
7. apology

Verbs

8. *embarrass*
9. disagree
10. weigh
11. surprise
12. prepare
13. calm
14. apologize

Adjectives

15. *embarrassed*
16. disagreeable
17. weighty
18. surprising
19. prepared
20. calming, calm
21. apologetic
22. prepared
23. disagreeable
24. surprised
25. weigh
26. apologetic
27. embarrassment

Exercise 2 page 40

1. c
2. e
3. f
4. g
5. h
6. b
7. d
8. a

Lesson E: Writing

Exercise 1 page 41

1. Carlos is the manager at a discount store; Ted is an employee in customer service.
2. at the discount store
3. Ted was criticized by Carlos because he acted rudely.
4. Yes. Carlos gently told him what he was doing wrong, and he told him something positive first.
5. He responded well to it. He said that he would work on being friendlier in the future.
6. He improved his customer service skills.

Exercise 2 page 41
Answers will vary.

Unit 9: The right attitude

Lesson A: Listening

Exercise 1 page 42
#3 is the main idea.

Exercise 2 page 42

1. *Adjusting Your Attitude for Success*
2. enjoyment / our daily tasks
3. Positive people / generally upbeat
4. a solution / every problem
5. a pleasure / be around
6. negative people / smile or laugh
7. Do you / anybody like that
8. Nobody / totally positive / totally negative
9. adjust your attitude
10. more successful life

Lesson B: Adverb clauses of concession

Exercise 1 page 43

1. *Even though Jeffrey makes a lot of money, he doesn't like his job.*
   Jeffrey doesn't like his job even though he makes a lot of money.
2. Although Sally has a difficult life, she remains positive about the future.
   Sally remains positive about the future although she has a difficult life.
3. Even though Jackson has a lot of friends, he sometimes feels depressed.
   Jackson sometimes feels depressed even though he has a lot of friends.
4. Although Shirley criticizes people a lot, she doesn't like it when people criticize her.
   Shirley doesn't like it when people criticize her although she criticizes people a lot.
5. Even though Rajiv attended the motivational speaker's lecture, he didn't feel inspired.
   Rajiv didn't feel inspired even though he attended the motivational speaker's lecture.

Exercise 2 page 43
Answers will vary. Possible answers:

1. I still find time to visit my grandparents
2. I'm learning it by studying a little at a time
3. I really like my class / is strict
4. speak Spanish in class, I try to speak only English
5. it is also exciting
6. Rachana / she misses her country

Lesson C: Reading

Exercise 1 page 44
Nouns

1. *idyll*
2. invasion
3. challenge
4. discouragement
5. determination
6. support
7. adoration
8. interaction

Verbs

9. *NA (does not exist)*
10. invade
11. challenge
12. discourage
13. determine
14. support
15. adore
16. interact

Adjectives
17. idyllic
18. invasive
19. challenging, challenged
20. discouraged, discouraging
21. determined, determining
22. supportive
23. adorable
24. interactive

Exercise 2 page 44
The following time phrases should be underlined:

"12 years ago," "one day five years ago," "two months," "five years later," "following his surgery," and "today"

Timeline should be filled in like this:

12 years ago: *Hugo came to the United States*

one day five years ago: he learned he had invasive prostate cancer or his idyllic world turned upside down

two months: he spent recovering

five years later: he is working and enjoying life

following his surgery: he took several positive steps to speed up his recovery

today: he works and volunteers with charities to help raise awareness about cancer

Lesson D: Reading
Exercise 1 page 45
Parts of speech
9. *adjective*
10. verb
11. adjective
12. noun
13. noun
14. verb
15. verb
16. adjective

Definitions
17. dismal, dark, or dreary
18. make impure or corrupt by contact or mixture
19. corrupted
20. failure to appear, especially for work or school
21. the act of stealing
22. get rid of or take away completely
23. fight against
24. poisonous

Exercise 2 page 45
Topic sentences
1. *Meet Nelly.*
2. Some psychologists even have a name for their negative attitude – "negativitis."
3. The causes of negativitis can be complex.
4. Just one person's negative attitude can be enough to contaminate the atmosphere of an entire office or group.
5. Although management should take an active role in solving the problem of workplace negativity, you, as an employee, can also take steps to combat the toxic effects of negativitis in your workplace or group.

Lesson E: Writing
Exercise 1 page 46
Introductory statement:
I am very interested in studying in Costa Rica for several reasons.

Concluding statement:
For all of these reasons, studying abroad in Costa Rica for a year definitely fits into my overall educational goals.

Transition words:
First of all, Secondly, My final reason

Exercise 2 page 46
Answers will vary.

Unit 10: Writing at work and school

Lesson A: Listening
Exercise 1 page 47
daily progress reports, work orders, shopping lists, restaurant orders, business reports

Exercise 2 page 47
1. *what your / is*
2. write daily / reports
3. from / 2010 report
4. that / full-time, career workers
5. probably / get hired
6. to make them / productive
7. will transfer / almost / job
8. more clearly / concisely

Lesson B: Causative verbs
Exercise 1 page 48
Suggested answers. Choice of causative may vary.

1. *Rachel had her students write an essay about their career goals last week.*
2. Rachel made her children clean up their bedrooms before their grandmother came over.
3. Rachel's neighbor had Rachel bring a potluck dish to her party.
4. Rachel got her husband to go to the opera with her.
5. Rachel made her daughter practice piano every day even though she didn't want to.

Exercise 2 page 48
Wording of answers will vary slightly.

1. *She had the students do some work*
2. She got them to start the project she had assigned them (before she went to the conference).
3. She had them throw their trash away.
4. She made them put the desks back in place.
5. She had them turn off their cell phones.
6. She made them listen to her.
7. She got them to use the computers only for class work.

Lesson C: Reading
Exercise 1 page 49
1. *vague*
2. savvy
3. seminar
4. essential
5. attachment
6. etiquette

Exercise 2 page 49
Wording will vary.

1. *The subject is vague.*
2. The email is mostly written in lowercase letters.
3. The email is too informal – she shouldn't write "lol" and "kinda" to her boss. She shouldn't use the salutation "hey sam."
4. She is sending a big email attachment.
5. She forwarded an email from her boss to other people.

Lesson D: Reading

Exercise 1 page 50

1. (don't get)
2. didn't read
3. easy
4. have to
5. most
6. immediately
7. clear
8. didn't skim

Exercise 2 page 50

Consequences

4. *It causes confusion for the reader who may not have time to read it in depth.*
5. Using the passive voice can cause confusion because the reader does not know who is doing what.
6. Fuzzy, abstract phrases cause readers to slow down and guess at their meanings.

Suggestions

7. Use short sentences and keep the language simple and familiar.
8. Use the active voice – it is more interesting and attention getting.
9. Use concrete, descriptive phrases to help readers form clear images in their minds.

Lesson E: Writing

Exercise 1 page 51

Problem

1. *Employees are leaving food in the refrigerator and forgetting about it. The lunchroom is smelly and unpleasant because the food in the refrigerator is rotting.*

Recommendations to correct the problem

2. Label your food with your name and the date.
Sign up to clean out the refrigerator twice a month.
Do not take anyone else's food out of the refrigerator.

Consequences if no action is taken

3. If you don't label your food, it wil be thrown out at the end of the day.
If you do not sign up to clean out the refrigerator or if you take someone else's food, you will lose your refrigerator privileges.

Timeline

4. The changes will be implemented immediately.

Exercise 2 page 51

Answers will vary.